The Bhagawadgita

N S Subrahmaniam

TARANG PAPERBACKS
a division of
VIKAS PUBLISHING HOUSE PVT LTD

VIKAS PUBLISHING HOUSE PVT LTD
576 Masjid Road, Jangpura, New Delhi 110014

Reprint, 1994

Printed at Rattan Enterprises. Delhi

Foreword

The *Bhagawadgita* stands out as a marvellous guide to man's ethical and moral life in this world and also in his journey in the realm of the Spirit. Its solutions and answers seem even more relevant to the present age, in which man, despite his achievements, despairs for happiness and peace. Sri Krishna unequivocally declares that even the most heinous sinner need not despair, if only he would open a new page in his book of life. An Upanishadic point stressed throughout the *Bhagawadgita* is that man can and should attain spiritual joy and serenity *in this work-a-day world and in this very body*. True wisdom consists of the knowledge of *both* the objective world *and* the subject himself.

Most of us are Arjunas, as we go about our worldly tasks, often baffled and rendered will-less by them. This novel presentation of the Song of God may be of use to the busy man of today.

SWAMI EKATMANANDA
President
Ramakrishna Asrama,
Ootacamund (Tamil Nadu)

Introduction

In the summer months of May-June 1976 I was on a *pada-yatra* from Bhopal to Allahabad for the *kumbha-mela*, along with the head of a religious *mutt*. I stopped at New Delhi on route. Here I ran into a lady of my acquaintance who has been reading the *Bhagawadgita* regularly. She said to me, "I have been reading the *Gita* regularly for a long time but I am not able to follow it fully—the Lord seems to speak too much of himself. Also the subject is changed too frequently."

I smiled and kept quiet, but at once remembered the predicament of Arjuna, who had said the very same thing ! "Oh Krishna! By these apparently conflicting words of yours you seem to confuse my understanding. Tell me precisely which one brings me the greatest good . . . ."

It was then that I thought of a re-arrangement of the *slokas* of the *Bhagawadgita*, a search for a more lucid pattern which would in no way disort the original text. This, then, is *not* the *Bhagawadgita* re-interpreted, but re-arranged.

I thank my son, Rajagopalan and my daughter-in-law, Girija for all the help they consistently rendered from beginning to end in the preparation, completion and revision of this work.

New Delhi   N. S. SUBRAHMANIAN

Contents

The Lord in His Immanence

Sri Krishna says: Arjuna, I am the primal cause of all creation and the eternal seed of all beings. There is nothing else besides Me. Even the gods and the great seers emanate from Me, and like many beads on a string all these are strung in Me.

I know the past, the present and the future. Yet neither the sages and gods, nor this world in delusion know Me as the unborn and immutable.

I am not manifest to all, because I am beyond all factors and forces, birthless and one without a beginning. Keeping My Prakriti under control, and through My own Yoga Maya, I manifest Myself;[1] and he who knows Me in truth and takes refuge in Me is freed from the recurring course of births and death.

All beings abide in Me, and all this world* is pervaded by Me alone in My unmanifest form, but I am not in them: nay, even those beings are not in Me, in truth.

Look at the wonderful power of My Yoga. Though the sustainer, creator and protector of all beings, in reality "My Self" does not dwell in them. It is only this much. Just as the all-pervading air always remains in ether, so too all this world is pervaded by Me only, in My unmanifest form.

Partha! I am the upholder of dharma. So whenever dharma

*The world is said to be sustained by men of virtue, the vedas, contented persons, those wedded to truth, philanthropists and good men.

declines and unrighteousness is on the ascent, and also when
there is a need for protection of the virtuous and destruction of
the evil-doers and re-establishment of dharma, I manifest Myself
of Myo wn free will.

I am ever glorious and divine in My incarnations, and he who
knows this truth, and understands as well, My supreme glory
and supernatural powers attains Me only, he is not reborn.

The Vibhuti

Arjuna says: Lord, I believe all that you say. You are the
Supreme Brahman[2] and the ultimate resort for all beings and the
holy of the holiest.

All the Sages and the celestial Sage Narada, also Asita, De-
vala and Vyasa glorify You as the eternal unborn and as the
resplendent omnipresent being. You too tell me so, but neither
the gods nor the spirits are fully aware of Your manifestations.

Purushottama! Oh God of gods! You are omniscient. So you
alone can rightly reveal to me your divine glories and their pre-
eminence in and among the created worlds and objects. So Pray,
tell me all that, and tell me also by what means I can constantly
remember You and meditate upon Your limitless magnificence.

The Lord replies: Partha, hear now! I am the Self (Atman)
residing in all. I am the source (creator), the middle (sustainer)
and the end (destroyer). There is nothing anywhere either moving
or stationary that exists without Me.

The seven great Seers (Marichi and others), the more ancient
four (Sanaka and others) and the fourteen "Manus" (progenitors
of mankind), all of them powerful and devoted to Me, are born
of My will.

Arjuna! I am Vishnu among the Adityas and the radiant Sun

among the luminaries. I am Marichi the glorious, among the Maruts and the moon among the stars.

I am Samaveda among the Vedas, Indra among the gods, mind among the sense-organs and consciouness in the living beings.

Of the Rudras I am Sankara; of the Yakshas and Rakshasas I am Kubera. I am Agni among the Vasus and Meru among the mountains.

Among priests I am Brihaspati: I am Skanda among warriors and among sheets of water I am the Ocean.

I am Bhrigu among the great seers, and of words I am the monosyllable "OM." Of Yajnas I am japa yajna[3] and among the sturdy immovables I am the Himalayas.

Of trees I am the Aswattha tree; of divine Sages Narada; I am "Chitra Ratha" among the celestial minstrels and Kapila the Saint among the Siddhas, or perfect souls.

Among horses I am Uchchaishravas; of lordly elephants I am Airavatha, and amongst men I am the king.

Of weapons I am the thunderbolt and among cows I am Kamadhenu; of poisonous snakes I am Vasuki; among aquatic beings I am Varuna. I am Aryaman among the manes, and Yama (god of death) among those that regulate, control and rule; and I am Ananta among non-venomous snakes.

Among the Daityas I am Prahlada; among reckoners I am Time. I am the lion among quadrupeds and Garuda among birds.

I am wind among elements that purify; I am Rama among the wielders of weapons; among fishes I am Makara, and among rivers I am the Ganges.

I am the productive passion, and among disputants in argument I am dispassionate reasoning. In the alphabet I am *akaram* which is also the first sound in OM; of compounds in grammar I am the cupulative compound.

I am the very sprout for everything that comes into being; I am the Goddess of wealth (Lakshmi) and the Goddess of learning (Saraswati) among women: I am the presiding deity over the forces and influences of steadfastness of mind, power of memory, intelligence and retention of memory and also fame and forbearance.

I am Brhatsamam in the vedic hymns, Gayatri in the mantras, Margasirsha in the months of the year, and of seasons of the year I am the spring.

I am the game of dice among those that deceive, the prowess of the powerful, and the victory of those victorious. I am effort and goodness (satvam) in good-natured people.

What Else Am I?

I am Vasudeva (Krishna) among the vrishnis and Arjuna among the pandavas: I am Vyasa of the Sages, and amongst the wise I am Sage Sukra (usana kavi).

I am the ruling power in the rulers; righteousness or right policy I am, for those aspiring victory; wisdom in the wise, and of secrets I am silence.

I am the sustainer of all and the universal dispenser of the fruits of action and justice. I am the all powerful and the inexorable force of death and eternal time.

I am sapidity in water: lustre in the Sun and moon: the sacred syllable OM in the Vedas, sound in either and prowess and enterprise in man which is rid of passion and attachment. I am pure odour in earth, brightness in fire, life in all beings and austerity in ascetics.

Arjuna! I am the power of intelligence in the intellect, and in the created worlds "the desire" which is in line with one's own duty and dharma. I am immortality[4] and death.[5] I am both existence (sat) and non-existence (asat).

Of all sciences, I am the science of the self (adhyatma vidya).

As the all-knowing I am the knower of the Vedas, the Vedantic traditions have their origin in Me. I am the vedic rituals, the sacrifices (Yajnas), the offerings to the departed ones, the herbage, and the food for the living beings. I am the sacred mantras, the sacrificial fire, clarified butter used in the offerings and verily also the very act of oblations into the fire.

I am the progenitor for this world, the mother, the sustainer, the grandsire, that which is "to be known," the holy one (purifier), the primal, sacred monosyllable OM, and likewise also the Vedas—the Rg, Yajus and Sama.

I am the Lord of all, the supreme goal, protector, friend and an unattached witness. I am the abode, an asylum, a retreat for those that surrender unto Me; the resting place and the repository into which all beings merge at the time of dissolution.

Penetrating the earth I support all the beings with My omnipotent power and as the moon myself, I cause the nourishment of all plants and vegetation.

As the digestive power (Vaisvanara) in the beings I digest the food with the Prana and Apana force. Memory and the loss of it are all of My influence

In the Sun I am radiation and heat. I hold back or send forth clouds and rain. From Me alone there emerges in the beings knowledge, memory, the loss of it, discrimination, sanity, forgiveness, forbearance, truthfulness, control of the sense-organs and mind, happiness and misery, evolution, and dissolution, fear and fearlessness, non-violence, equanimity, contentment, austerity, charity, fame and also ill-fame.

Whatever other entities there are of *satvic*, *rajasic* and *tamasic* nature, know them all as evolved from Me alone. In reality, however, I am not in them though they abide in Me.

I am the effulgence in the Sun which illumines the worlds and the light which the fire and the moon emit.

Arjuna! But of what use is it to you to know about all these, because whatever of the creation I pervade in My infinitude, "that" proclaims My glory or excellence, and whatever is suspicious, holy, divine and powerful, know them all as just as part only of My divine splendour.

[Arjuna is now desirous of beholding the Lord, the unknown and the unknowable in His cosmic form—Visvaroopa.]

The Cosmic Form Revealed

Arjuna says: Lord! I have just heard your words of wisdom and your glory, and I believe all that You say. I am rid of my ignorance too, and I desire to see You, the imperishable one in Your universal form.

I pray: If you think I am capable of beholding it, please do reveal that divine form also.

The Lord replies: Arjuna! See My multifarious divine forms in hundreds and thousands and in diverse colours and shapes.

Behold the twelve Adityas, the eight Vasus, the eleven Rudras, the twin-born Ashwinikumars, the Maruts, and see also the many more wonderful forms of Mine, never seen by you before —see this entire creation with all the movable and immovable objects and anything else you wish to see, all in Me.

But, as it would not be possible for you to see Me with your mortal eyes, I bestow unto you the celestial vision with which you can see My divine form and My power of Yoga.

Sanjaya says to Dhritarashtra: O King! Having spoken thus, Lord Hari revealed to Arjuna His divine form.

That resplendent form bedecked with wondrous garlands, apparels and ornaments, holding divine weapons in its hands and anointed with fragrance, was most bewildering and bewitching to the sight.

A poor, and at best a near comparison of this brilliant form could be the effulgence of a thousand Suns if they were to appear simultaneously in the skies.

Then Arjuna, the son of Pandu, saw the Infinite form in the very body of the Lord, the God of Gods.

Bowing his head Arjuna says: Lord! I see in Your person all the Gods and multitudes of different beings with Brahma, the creator, seated on His lotus seat.

I see You with many hands, mouths and eyes in Your Infinite form everywhere, but nowhere do I see Your beginning or the end.

I see You with the divine diadem, mace and Chakra and a dazzling immeasurable splendour all around Your person, blinding like a blazing Sun.

Yonder space, between heaven and earth, also every inch and corner here, all this is pervaded by You alone. Your form is mighty and marvellous, and seeing. It with numerous faces, eyes, and limbs O Mighty Lord, the worlds are terrified. So am I *

Lord! You are *that* which is and also *that* which is not You are again *that* which is beyond both the finite and the infinite.

You are the primal God, the ancient first-born, and the Supreme resort for this universe. You are the knower, the knowable and the highest abode. Verily, all this world is pervaded by You only, in Your Infinite form.

*Arjuna was bestowed with Divine vision, but he says "I am terrified." ...yt it is because only his "eyes" were divine in its powers to see what could not otherwise be seen with the mortal eyes of flesh; whilst, the heart of Arjuna remained the same old one, unchanged to display its likes and

You are Vayu, Yama, Agni, Varuna, the Moon, Brahma, the creator and also the parent of all.

You are of infinite prowess: You pervade everything, so You are everywhere and thus again, everything else.

> *Obeisance, Obeisance again, a thousand times . . .*
> *Salutations to You from front, from behind and*
> *from all around You, as You are omnipresent.*

You are the primeval being, the imperishable Supreme the One worthy of being known: You are the protector of the eternal Dharma and the ultimate resort for this world.

You are infinite and without a beginning and an end. The Sun and the Moon are your eyes, blazing fire Your mouth, and You scorch this universe by Your radiance.

Hosts of Gods, some of them frightened, enter your body and they praise You with salutations; other Sages extol You saying "Let there be Peace" and they also pray to You with sweet hymns.

The eleven Rudras, the twelve Adityas, eight Vasus and the manes and multitudes of Gandharvas, Yakshas, Siddhas and others—all look at you in awe.

I see the sons of Dhrtarashtra too, with hosts of other kings, Bhishma, Drona and Karna—and also the mighty warriors on our side rushing forth into your fearful mouths. As rivers flow towards the sea, as moths enter fire, so too they march unto You only, for their destruction. I see some of them sticking in the interstices of your teeth with their smashed heads.

O Lord! Your fierce glow scorches all on all sides, and I see you licking them as You swallow them through your mouths of flame.

O Vishnu! Seeing Your effulgent form with a wide open mouth and large shining eyes reaching even the heavens, like a raging fire of destruction that engulfs worlds at the time of dissolution, I know not even the cardinal points. I am frightened: bewildered I am, and I have not peace or fortitude.

O Lord! Be kind and merciful. O great God! Again Salutations to You. Be pleased. I wish to know You, the Primal being in its essence for as it is, with a terrible looking form, I know not who You are, and what your present disposition is.

The Lord assuages. He says: Arjuna! I am the baffling Time and I am here for annihilation. Know that even without You all these warriors have already been slain by Me, and that you are going to be a mere instrument.

Therefore, arise, fight and conquer them all and attain the glory and sovereignty of an affluent kingdom.

Sanjaya to Dhritarashtra: On hearing these words of the Lord, Arjuna spoke to him in a faltering voice.

Arjuna says: It is natural that the world glorifies You and bows down to You, and the demoniac ones, getting frightened, flee in all directions.

O Lord! O noble of the noblest and of unrivalled glory . . . O Infinite Lord of the celestials! and, the progenitor of Brahma, the creator, and abode of the Universe! so why would they not salute You? There is none equal to you anywhere. You are the great teacher of the worlds, the father of all the moving and unmoving worlds; and the most adorable being, worthy of the worthiest, for, how can there be one greater than you?

Not realizing this greatness of Yours, whatever I might have said importunately out of ignorance or affection, hailing You as "Ae Krishna . . . Ae Yadava," and in whatever way You might have been slighted by me in jest, while at play, when in bed, or while sitting or dining, either alone or in company, all that I entreat You, My Lord, to forgive.

I entreat You to be gracious. Just as a father forgives the lapses of his son, a friend condones the faults of his friend and a lover excuses his beloved one, even so, forgive me O Lord!

Lord! I am delighted to see what has never been seen by me before; at the same time there is fear in my mind. Pray! therefore, reveal Yourself to me ... and let me see that old form of Yours with your mace, disc and diadem.

The Lord says, Arjuna! Be not afraid on seeing this terrible form of mine. Rid of your fear, and with a cheerful mind, see Me again with My conch, chakra, mace and lotus.

He then assumes His benign form and gladdens Arjuna, who says: "Janardana—Seeing You in this form, as before, I am well-composed."

The Lord further says: Arjuna! I have revealed to you this Divine Infinite form through My own Supreme Yogic power. It is exceedingly difficult for one to see Me thus, as you have done. Even the Gods are ever eager to behold this form which has not been seen by any before.

Partha! Neither by a study of the vedas, nor by performance of rituals, sacrifices and austerities, nor by offering of gifts and the like am I visible in this form as now seen by you: but it is only by single-minded devotion that I can be seen in this form, known in actual practice and courted in mutual friendship.

And it is he who is constantly established in the "Path of devotion" that attains immortality and bliss transcending all.

The Path of Devotion

The Lord says: Arjuna! That paramount state in which all beings rest, and that supreme being by whom all this is pervaded is attainable by single-minded devotion (bhakti).[6]

And I speedily rescue from the ocean of transmigratory existence beset with birth and death those pious devotees who constantly worship Me with devotion also surrendering unto Me the fruits of their actions.

Partha! Am I not the abode of even Brahma (the creator), of immortality, of everlasting virtue and unending Bliss?

So remaining unattached, hold on to Me in devotion and hold Me as the supreme goal. Have no hatred or malice towards anyone. Dedicate your work as well to Me. And that way, and in that state, you are dear to Me and you attain Me.

Raising a doubt Arjuna says: Lord! As between those devotees who adore You devoutly and those others who worship the imperishable unmanifest supreme Brahman, who is the best?

The Lord replies: Of all I consider those who keep their minds ever on Me and worship Me devoutly with supreme faith to be the best of the Yogis.

However, even the others who are self-controlled, even-minded and devoted to doing good to all living beings and who adore the eternal all-pervading unmanifest Brahman which is beyond all comprehension attain Me.

But this path to the unmanifest is more rugged, and it is attained only with difficulty by an embodied being. Therefore,

Arjuna, resort to the Yoga of equanimity: resign mentally all actions to Me, fix your mind and intellect on Me alone. When you abide in Me only, I redeem you from the course of repeated births and deaths.

If, however, you are unable to do so, then seek to attain Me by the Yoga of a sustained practice of your choice. If you are unable to take up this course, then be intent on performing "actions solely for my sake."

Again, if you are unable to resort to this Yoga of actions, or actions for My sake, then take refuge in Me in self-control, renounce the fruits of all actions in My favour, because this is by far the best.

Dhananjaya! Whilst knowledge is superior to mere practice without a proper understanding and insight, meditation is superior to knowledge, *but* it is the "renunciation of the fruits of action" that is superior still the last step in the ladder—for, peace* follows instantly from such renunciation.

Buddhi Yogam

Arjuna! Men of wisdom devoutly worship Me with their mind, intellect and their very lives on Me. Knowing Me as the Supreme they sing My glory, propagate same amongst themselves in a spirit of service, and remain a happy lot in this way of life and pursuit deriving the bliss of their devotion.

Just to bless them I dwell in the hearts of those ever devoted to Me in their worship and love: Of My own, I dispel the darkness of their ignorance by the Light of Knowledge. I shower My

---

*Peace and Bliss. They refer to an inexplicable state of "unified super consciousness and supreme existence." It is not a mere quietude of the mind, either. It is not also a mere cessation of activities: it is not the happiness or peace that deep sleep gives. It is something more deep, vital and positive the effects and meaning of which have to be experienced, rather than expressed. In fact, it is a *real* existence which is not within the realms of speech and (expression).

grace upon them, and in that illumined state of total integration, the Yoga of the intellect (Buddhi Yogam), they attain Me only.

Who is Dear to Me?

The Lord says: Dhananjaya! Alike to pain and pleasure, friend and foe, honour and dishonour, good and evil, praise and censure, heat and cold; forgiving by nature, of firm resolve, free from malice and ego, friendly, compassionate, self-controlled, contemplative and ever contented; mind set on Me and self dedicated to Me—such a person is dear to Me.

The pious one from whom others get no trouble, and he who gets no trouble, either, from the world; the one who is equanimous and free from elation, anger, fear, anxiety and all other mental afflictions; one who neither desires, nor rejoices, nor hates or grieves; who is impartial, craves not but continues to perform the ordained duties—who is dexterous, pure internally and externally, has no particular attachment to home (being thereby free to move about anywhere, at any time with ease, in an unencumbered manner without attachment)—such a person is dear to Me.

Surely, those, with faith and fervour, who take recourse to this path of Devotion, and actually practice this Science of high spiritual value, keeping Me as their supreme goal are also very dear to Me.

Arjuna! Whoever offers Me with sincere love[7] a leaf, a flower, a fruit or even water for that matter—that I delightfully partake of.

So, offering unto Me by way of love, devotion and dedication whatever you do, eat or give away as gift—be rid of the good and evil consequences of actions (Karma): and On Me fix thy mind: to Me bring thy devotion: to Me make thy obeisance; by this way, to Me, indeed, thou shalt surely come.

Who Resorts to Him?

Dhananjaya! People who resort to me are of four types; the afflicted, the spiritual aspirants the material seekers and the enlightened ones. All of them are noble, but of these, the enlightened one, over attached to Me in single-minded devotion (Yoga) is the best, (because he is in constant communion with Me).

To Him I am very dear; indeed, and he is also dear to Me. In fact, I regard him as My very Self, because he has taken refuge in Me alone with his mind fixed on Me as the highest goal, fully aware all the time, after many births, that *Vasudeva*, is everything.* Such a Mahatman is indeed rare to come across.

[After this meditation upon the glory of the Lord, we revert to the baltte-field at Kurukshetra.]

---

*The principle of surrender—Saranagadi is evident here. Further, as is very well proclaimed, the Lord does not ever reject one who surrenders unto Him with all faith and sincerity.

Kurukshetra

Addressing Sanjaya, Dhritarashtra said: What did my sons and those of Pandu do, after all of them assembled at the holy plains of the Kurukshetra battlefield?

Sanjaya replied: King Duryodhana saw in front of him the army of the Pandavas drawn up for the battle, and then spoke to his preceptor Drona as follows.

My revered Guru! Behold the vast army of the Pandavas arrayed by your disciple, the son of Drupada. Here, on our side, are heroes equal to Bhima and Arjuna, such as Satyaki, Virata and Draupada, Dhrishtaketu, Chekitana, the valiant king of Kasi and Purujit, Kuntibhoja, and Saibya.

Yudhamanyu, the valiant Uttamaujan, Abhimanyu, the son of Subhadra and the five sons of Drupada are all mighty warriors —Maha Rathas!

Also know about the distinguished warriors on our side. They are yourself, Karna, Kirpa, Aswatthama, Vikarna and Bhurisravas. There are also other heroes here, skilled in warfare and determined to give up their lives for me.

This army of ours protected by Bhishma is insufficient, but the army of the Pandavas is sufficient for their victory. Therefore, from all sides, and from your respective positions, you all have to protect Bhishma in particular.

p35 BGAII

Then Bhishma, the Kuru patriarch cheered Duryodhana, thundering forth and blowing his conch. Trumpets and horns rounded at the battlefront resulting in a tumultuous noise.

At this time, Sri Krishna and Arjuna, who were seated on a glorious chariot drawn by white horses, blew their conches "Panchajanya" and "Devadattam" while Bhima blew his mighty one "Paundram."

King Yudhishtira, Nakula, Sahadeva and the others also blew their respective conches making the heaven and earth to resound as well, and this great sound rent the hearts of Dhritarashtra's sons too

At this stage Arjuna said to Sri Krishna as follows: O Achuta, drive in my chariot to a suitable place between the two armies from where I can clearly see those arrayed in battle, and those with whom I have to fight.

Sri Krishna then positioned his chariot accordingly in front of Bhishma, Drona and other kings and said: Partha, behold these Kauravas assembled here.

Arjuna saw in both the armies his relations—uncles, brothers, cousins, fathers-in-law, preceptors, friends, well wishers and others for whom his veneration was ever due, and then, over-whelmed with grief, he spoke to Sri Krishna as follows:

Lord! On seeing these kinsmen here ready for a battle, I fail and falter. My mouth is parched up, my body quivers, my skin burns all over the body, my mind reels, as it were, and there is horripilation. The bow (Gandiva) drops from my hand, and I am not able even to stand.

O Kesava! The omens are bad and I see no good in killing my own kith and kin in battle. I desire neither victory, nor kingdom, nor pleasure.

Govinda! Of what use are all these, or even life itself to me? Because those very persons for whose sake we covet the throne, luxury and pleasures are arrayed here, all of them staking their lives and possessions on earth.

I do not want to kill them even if they should kill me—no, not even for the sovereignty of the three worlds, much less for that of this earth.

Lord! When there is a destruction of the family, the time honoured traditions (dharma) are lost: When unrighteousness (adharma) thus becomes the way of life, the women in the family become corrupt, and they lose their honour, and from this degraded state there is an intermixture of caste.

This calamity leads both the society and the destroyers of the race as well to hell; further, the manes suffer, for they are deprived of *sraddha* and *tarpana* (the ceremonial offerings of lumps of cooked rice and water to the departed souls).

This havoc spreads further, from the family to the society at large, and all such persons who have lost the family traditions are doomed for eternal Hell.

Alas! We are going to be the perpetrators of such heinous crimes due to our lust for power and kingdom, and out of greed for the joys of life, now that we are intent on killing our own kinsmen.

So it does not behove us to kill these kinsmen of ours. How can we be happy if we annihilate our own men? What joy can we derive by slaying the sons of Dhritarashtra? Sin alone we will acquire if we kill them.

Although these desperadoes blinded by greed do not themselves see the evil of destruction of one's own race and the inherent sin involved in enmity towards friends, why should not we, who see them all right, turn away from that unholy path?

Lord! If the sons of Dhritarashtra now facing us in battle should slay me, even when I am unarmed and unresisting, that would be far better for me.

Sanjaya to Dhritarashtra: Speaking thus, grief stricken, Arjuna put aside his bow and arrows and sat down on the chariot as though exhausted.

Seeing Arjuna thus in deep distress Krishna spoke.

Arjuna! How is it that an ignominious infatuation, a weakness of heart unbecoming of the brave which brings neither fame nor heavens has come over you in this crisis?

It is unworthy of you. Yield not to unmanliness.

Shake off this petty faint-heartedness: Arise and Act.

Confused, Arjuna, continuing his erroneous predilections says: O Madhusudana! Bhishma and Drona are worthy of veneration. How shall I fight such great men worthy of respect?

Krishna! As between killing them and living in the world, I think that, without killing these noble-minded elders, it would be far better to live on alms; because, by killing them I shall only be inheriting stained wealth and deriving sordid pleasure.

Lord! I do not know which of the two is better—for us to conquer the sons of Dhritarashtra, those very persons killing whom we would not desire to live in this world, *or* for them to conquer us. (Anything may happen: we may be vanquished, or we may be victorious.)

And now the heat of my grief is so devastating that it is drying up my senses. Even if I am to obtain an undisputed sovereignty over others, an affluent kingdom on earth, and a lordship over the Gods, I do not still see that, which would alleviate my sorrow. With my natural traits overrun by the vice of faint-heartedness, and overcome by helplessness and sin, I am puzzled, and I do not know what to do and what my duty (dharma) is.

Lord! Pray, I ask you. Tell me that which will be of definite good to me. I am Your disciple, and I have taken refuge in You. Instruct me in the matter. Saying these words, Arjuna lapsed into silence.

Sanjaya to Dhritarashtra. Having spoken to Sri Krishna thus, Arjuna again said to him: "I will not fight."

p 86 : B6AII

The Self

The Lord spoke as follows to Arjuna who was in sorrow in between the two armies.

Arjuna! You grieve for those who should not be grieved for; yet you speak words of wisdom. Know that the wise grieve not either for the dead or for the living.

Nature (prakriti) under the divine command is the cause for this body, but verily a part of Myself presides over the sense-organs, (as with others), to enliven them, and it is said to cause the conditioned Self to enjoy the sense objects.

Just as a breeze carries with it odour from its seat, so too does the embobied Soul move with its latent desires from one body to another with the senses as well.

The deluded ones, though striving, do not perceive this Truth: they do not see the Self (Atman) either when He resides in or departs from this body. It is only the Yogis and others with pure wisdom that revel in this truth and in the revelation within.

Partha! The senses are said to be superior to their objects; superior to those is the mind; but superior to the mind is the intellect, while what is superior to the intellect is the Self (Atman).

The Self (Atman) is not born: nor does it die at any time—it is birthless, eternal, everlasting and ancient. The body may be slain but not so the soul.

It is not, indeed, that I did not exist at any time, nor you, nor these things; nor that we all shall not exist hereafter.

The unreal has no existence and the real (Atman) never ceases to be. None can bring about the destruction of this indestructible core, and this is the finality arrived at by the learned seekers of Truth.

Arjuna! Know the Self (Atman)[8] by which all this is pervaded, and perceived too, as the imperishable. Just as the all-pervading ether is not contaminated by reason of its subtlety, so too is the Self in the body not contaminated.

O Descendant of Bharata! This embodied Self, (Atman) in all beings, is eternally indestructible.

The Self (Atman) is eternal, imperishable and infinite; it is only the physical body, or the manifestation of this indestructible phenomenon that dies, because, that alone has had a birth and a beginning. Therefore "fight." So you ought not to grieve on this account.

He who thinks the Self (Atman) to be a slayer and also he who thinks it is slain, both are ignorant of the Truth. The Self neither slays nor is it slain. How, and by whom, then, will a person who knows this Soul (Atman) to be immortal, eternal and imperishable, cause this to be slain?

If, however, you should think that the Self (Atman) is in the grips of perpetual birth and death, even then you ought not to grieve, because, death is certain to one who is born and to one who dies, re-birth is sure to be. Over this inevitable fact you ought not to grieve.

All beings were unmanifest in the beginning, have become manifest in between and will be unmanifest again, on dissolution. Why lament over the inevitable?

Just as a person discards his worn out clothes for new ones, so does an embodied Soul cast off its mortal coil at death. *p 104*

p 90 -100 B6 A I I

Again, even as an embodied Soul attains different stages in its physical growth—such as childhood, youth and old age—so too does it attain another body: wise men are not deluded about this.

p106

Weapons do not cleave the Self (Atman), fire does not burn it; water does not drench it and wind does not dry it up. So the Self (Atman) in you is incapable of being cut, of being burnt, and is impervious to water—it is eternal, all-pervading, stable, immovable and primordial. It is unmanifest and immutable; it is beyond comprehension.* Knowing it to be such, you ought not to grieve. p108

The Self (*Atman*) *is a non-doer* (*akarta*)[9]

The Lord says: Arjuna! It is *all nature* that functions. The Lord does not determine for the people and the world, either doership, the agency for actions, *or* actions as such, *or* the union of these with the fruits of actions.

So he who mistakenly considers his own self to be an agent or doer is of a perverse type. He is a wayward, far from truth, and one deluded.

He who knows the Self as a non-doer" understands it right, and he becomes free.

In such a non-egoistic state of an oneness of understanding and experience, though one kills, he does not really kill, nor is he bound. (That is, he is not bound by the effects of even the most heinous crimes in that supreme state.)

Arjuna! This state of self-realization is difficult to achieve, so one perceives this Self (Atman) as a marvel; scarce another speaks of it as a marvel, and scarce still another hears of it as a wonder, whilst there are yet some, who know it not, even after

*It is beyond comprehension but it is also stated that it is yet capable of being perceived and experienced in the cavity of the heart *by* and *in* a pure and serene mind in introspection and intution.

hearing about it.

Creation[10]

Arjuna! At the end of every cycle[11] of creation, all beings attain My *prakriti,* and at the beginning of the next I send them forth including the creator.

Presiding over My nature, I repeatedly send forth this conglomeration of animate and inanimate beings of a pattern now, as it originally was, and they helplessly emerge according to their pre-natal tendencies* when the Creator's day starts, and they all dissolve in Him, when night sets in.

Dhananjaya! But creation does not bind Me, because I remain unattached.

All embodied beings emanate from the unmanifest at the commencement of the Creator's day; and at the commencement of night, they merge in the same subtle body of the Creator, and the unmanifest. Beyond this unmanifest there is yet another eternal Unmanifest—that Supreme Divine Being which does not perish, even when all other beings perish.

The imperishable unmanifest (Aksharam) is my abode (Param Sthanam), attaining which, one does not return to this world of transmigratory existence any more.

Partha! Those who know the Creator's day are the knowers of day and night.

The Lord says: Arjuna! This mortal life in the created world is like a peepul tree. Curiously its roots are said to be the Primal Being above; the stem is said to be the Creator (Brahma) and the leaves are the holy scriptures (Vedas).

The branches of this tree in the shape of the different species

*The pre-natal tendencies are the "vasanas," the latent unseen effects of actions (Karma), which form the "base" for the later "sprout."

of living beings nourished by the three modes of nature (Gunas), and having the sense-objects for their tender leaves extend both downwards and upwards: its roots are stretched below, leading to actions which bind the embodied Soul.

Its nature, or form as such, is not perceivable here. It has neither a beginning, nor an end, nor even stability. So, cutting down this Peepul tree, the roots of which are so deeplaid with the formidable weapon of dispassion, overcoming the evils of attachment, free from pride and delusion, ever devoted to spiritual pursuits, rid of desires and the pairs of opposites such as pleasure and pain, one should diligently seek that Supreme Being, mentally alert all the time, and exclaiming to himself.

"I seek refuge in that primal person from whom has emanated this unending creation. . ."

and on reaching Him one does not return to this world, any more, because he has finally attained that Supreme Being only.

The Sun does not illumine that region, nor the Moon nor the Fire. *That* is My Supreme state, reaching which there is no return—repeats the Lord.

The perishable and the imperishable

Arjuna! There are two beings (Purushas) in this world—the created perishable beings (Ksharam or Adhibhutam) immutable and the Imperishable (Aksharam) Purusha or Brahmam. Its manifestation as the soul force (Atman) in the created beings is Adhyatman.

Different from these is the Supreme Person who, interpenetrating the three worlds, sustains them all. He is the Universal Soul (Paramatman).

Since I am beyond the perishable (Ksharam) and greater than the imperishable (Aksharam) I am venerated in this world, and in the scriptures (Vedas) as the Supreme Being (Purushottama).

The Supreme Person (Purusha) in this body, though really

transcendent, is the witness, the protector, the sustainer, the Lord, the Lord of Lords (the immutable). He is a dispassionate witness (Sakshi) existing in, and illumining instantly, and all the time, cognition and recognition.

Although an indweller in our body without a beginning, an end and attributes, this Supreme Self (Paramatman) neither acts nor gets attached.

Arjuna! An undeluded person who knows Me as the all-pervading Supreme, worships Me alone, with a total awareness that I am all.

O Sinless one! This is a sacred doctrine now expounded by Me to you. Knowing this one becomes wise and accomplished are all his duties in his life.

The one who, unswervingly rejoices in his own self in a state of enlightenment attains all satisfaction and full contentment: He has nothing to gain by performance of actions, nor lose anything on account of nonperformance. So he has no duties to perform, and the mission of his life is fulfilled.

Partha! Know that he has consummated his existence in this world, having reached the highest goal of life.

The field and the knower of the field

The Lord says: Arjuna! Whatever is manifest in this world, animate or inanimate, know that to be the outcome of a mystic order of the union of both matter and spirit (Kshetra and Kshetrajnan). The Kshetra in brief, is this body consisting of the five subtle elements, the ego, intellect and the unmanifest primordial matter; the ten sense-organs, mind and the five sense-objects (of sound, touch, colour, taste and smell)—also desire, aversion, happiness and misery and the life principle.

And that which is conscious of it is Myself—the Kshetrajnan. It is the Jeevatman in all the *Kshetras*. I am that Jeevatman, the knower of the field, the embodied Self, seated in the hearts of all.

The primordial matter is the Mother and I am the Father. The *Prakriti*, or nature in her primordial, undeveloped state is the womb, and in that I place the seed of Consciousnes—so the father I am: and from this follows the combination of Matter and Spirit, of the birth and beginning of all beings.

Partha! It is the knowledge of the Kshetra and Kshetrajnan (of Prakriti), and of Purusha, (of matter and spirit) which I consider to be good knowledge.

This Truth has been eulogized in the Vedic hymns, and in the passages indicative of the Supreme Being (Brahman).

Just as the one Sun illumines this world, even so O Descendent of Bharata, does the emdodied Soul (Kshetri)* illumine the field of his and achievents (Kshetram).

And such ones attain the Supreme who wisely perceive this Truth and the difference between Matter or field (Kshetram) and Spirit or knower of the field (Kshetrajnan) and negation of matter (Prakriti) with her evolutes and freedom of the created beings from the cause (nature).

*This embodied Soul is "microcosmic (Jivatman): and as a "macrocosmic" phenomenon it is the universal Soul (Paramatman).

The Path of Action

The Lord says: Arjuna! The scriptures (Vedas) which deal with the triple aspects of nature speak also about actions (Karma), and I will now tell you all about this glorious path for you to tread: but an apparent incongruity is, this Science is a baffling one even to the learned ones, who are sometimes in doubt as to what action and inaction are.

Yoga is dexterity in action. There is something for you to know about actions prescribed and about inaction. But at the end of it all; in your illumined state, you will find that these very actions are powerless to act, they having lost their "binding effects" upon you.

Partha! To start with, those impelled by results are miserable and wretched; to work alone you have the right, not to the fruits thereof.

Hear Me again, on Karma (actions).[12] Ultimately they are the results of the three modes of nature (Prakriti); and so it is only a deluded mind that thinks "I am the doer."

One does not reach a "state of freedom from action" just because he has abstained from performance of actions; nor attain a "state of perfection" by mere renunciation of actions (Sanyas).

O Son of Kunti! As actions motivated by desire are far inferior to those performed with an equanimity of mind, resort to this technique, and discharge your duties efficiently without attachment.

Men of selfless actions (karma yogins) give up attachment and perform their duties (with the body, mind and intellect) solely for purposes of mental purification.

And on yourself acquiring that knowledge and skill, you will see for yourself the oneness of all beings in you, as well as in Me too, even when you should be in the the midst of the performance of various actions is your daily life.

You will be led to perfection in actions, that way, as you are otherwise bound by their effects if you are going to be engaged in actions for your own sake, or in the performance of those other than a sacrifice.

Arjuna! Therefore with a constant awareness *I am the Self* (Atman), and also with a knowledge of the Self (*Atma Jnana*) which is freed from its cravings and desires and your other notions of ownership and possessions, rid also of your mental and emotional upsurge, fight, be e ngaged in actions, dedicating mentally all such actions to Me'.

On action, renunciation of action, inaction and the rest.

Arjuna addresses the Lord. Krishna! You extol the Path of renunciation (Sanyas) and the Path of Action as well. Tell me precisely that which is good for me.

The Lord replies: Arjuna! Renunciation of actions and performance of actions—both are good, and they lead to the same goal. But performance of actions is superior to renunciation, because that ideal state of renunciation of actions is difficult to achieve without Yoga in action.

And as between the three—pure inactivity, just staying away from the field of activity, as though withdrawing from the scene of actions, renunciation of actions (Karma Sanyas), and performance of actions, the last is the best. Why?

The Lord says: If you desist from actions, is it not that you cannot even maintain your body? Also, is it not that none can remain inactive even for a moment, because everyone is help-lessly driven to the field of actions by his own inborn tendencies (vasanas) and his nature-born qualities (Prakriti)? Therefore perform the prescribed duties because action is superior to inaction.

Partha! As for "renunciation," it is not possible for the em-bodied beings to completely disown all actions as such; so, he who relinquishes "the fruits of action" is indeed a true relinqui-sher (Thyagi).

In the end, know that all beings follow their nature, and that wisemen too act, according to their own disposition[13] because of 'atent tendencies. So what can restraint alone easily do?

¹ ⁱe basis for all actions

Partha! Know from Me the five contributory causes for the accomplishment of actions, good, bad, physical, vocal or mental.

They are this body, as the seat of all actions; the agent as the doer in you; the different sense organs the divergent activities you perform and the *presiding Divinty in you.*

The threefold impluse to action are knowledge the knowable and the knower.

The three bases for action are the instruments of action—senses and perception, action[14] itself and the *doer.*

The fourfold division of duties

Arjuna! I have formulated a fourfold division of work for men in the Society. They are the qualities of a Brahmin—sere-nity, self-control, austerity, purity, forbearance, uprightness, faith, knowledge and realization—and also the belief that there is a life after death i.e. one after this present life (Asthikyam)—(can also be stated as belief in God, the scriptures, and the other world).

Take a small reservoir and a vast lake. All the purpose that a small reservoir serves is very well served by a vast lake entirely filled with water.

Now the known Vedas against that which is beyond the known. Likewise, the purpose which the Vedas serve in the field of mere knowledge is more than well served by a man of realization, in his *overflowing state* of an *oneness of experience.*

p133

Heroism. boldness, firmness, bravery, not fleeing from the battlefield, generosity and lordliness are the duties of the warrior class—Kshatrias. For them, it is said, there is nothing more welcome than a righteous war.

Agriculture, cattle-rearing and trade are the duties of the Vaishya.

Work in the nature of service is the duty of others.

This fourfold division of Society was ushered in by Me according to the aptitudes of men. Though I am the originator of this scheme, know Me not to be the agent therefor, because I am a non-doer, the immortal Lord.

Duty

Arjuna! Devotion to one's own duty is glorified. It leads one to perfection and it is as efficacious as worshipping the Lord, from whom all this creation has emanated, and by whom all this is pervaded.

Though devoid of merit, better is one's own duty than that of another well performed; as by this one incurs no sin or evil.

One's own duty, though devoid of merit, is preferable to that of another well performed. Even death, (if it should come, per chance, in the discharge of one's own duty) brings him blessedness, because there is a sense of fear and apprehension in the minds of those that perform the duties of another.

Do not therefore relinquish your own duty, though same may be attended with evil. It is not that all work and undertakings, for that matter, are tainted with some blemish or other, as fire is by smoke?

Arjuna! Just as the ignorant ones perform their duties with attachment, even so the wisemen should perform actions unattached, in the larger interests of the world. Janaka and others of his type attained perfection by actions alone of this unattached nature. Men of perfect knowledge should not straight away try to unsettle the belief of those attached to the sense objects and deluded by the modes of Prakriti (nature). Instead, he should perform actions himself intently, and get others also sincerely devoted to work.

The Lord repeats: Why that? Even from the point of view of a proper world order, you should discharge your duties only that way

There is nothing for Me to do here and in the three worlds: also there is nothing worth attaining by Me, but remaining unattained. Yet, I continue to work. Why? Because, if ever I cease to be so engaged in action, people will follow my path in every way. They will be misled, and there will be confusion and disorder all round. Know that, whatever a great man does, the others copy that: and whatever he accepts as authority, that also the generality of the men follow.

Arjuna! He who knows the truth about the respective spheres of action and nature (the modes of Prakriti), holding that it is only the Gunas (in the shape of the sense-organs and the mind) that rest in the Gunas again, as the sense objects of perception and experience, such a person does *not* get attached to them, and he is *not* bound.

Arjuna in doubt addresses the Lord: He says: Lord! Though unwilling, yet as though impelled by force a person commits sin. What is the compulsion here?

The Lord answers. Desire and wrath are born of *Rajo guna* (one of the modes of Prakriti). They are the enemies, here, sinful in nature and have to be shunned. As fire by smoke, mirror by dust; embryo by the amnion, even so is true knowledge covered by this. Know that it is an eternal enemy of the wise.*

Who are not bound by actions?

Arjuna! Though ever in action, the self-controlled seekers of truth who experience the same life principle everywhere, who are pure in mind and integrated in Yoga, who identify the other beings in their own Self and remain unaffected—such ones are *not* bound by their actions.

And, as for himself, the Lord says: Actions do not bind Me. Nor do I desire their fruits. And, he who knows Me thus is also not bound.

He further says: Even the ancient seekers of liberation discharged their duties this way. You too fall in line, take refuge in Me; do your duty as done by them, and attain My eternal and imperishable state through My grace, though ever performing actions.

Ever contented with what chance brings, free from jealousy and the pair of opposites, balanced in success and failure, without a refuge, renounce your attachment to the fruits of action and remain unattached in the world. Then you are also a non-doer (akarta) though in the midst of actions: and in that situation you are *not* bound by their effects.

Unattached men of pure knowledge who discharge their ordained duties as a sacrifice only, without definite expectation of results, or as an offering to the Lord with their minds well established in the path and pursuit, are those whose actions melt away—they are innocuous.

Similar is the case, and no evil befalls him, continues the Lord, in the case of those who have renounced the fruits of their actions through Yoga, whose doubts have been dispelled by knowledge and, more important, who have learnt to relax, revel

*The Lord also says—(Chap: XVI. 21) Passion, anger and greed are the triple gateways to Hell and to destruction of one's own being (Self) They are to be shunned.

and remain rooted in their own Self. In all these cases Actions do not bind them all—they melt away, He says.

A Karma Yogi in his actions and experiences,
and on freedom from actions

Arjuna! Yoga is dexterity in action. Endowed with this knowledge you will be rid of both the good and the evil effects of actions, and freed from the shackles of bondage as well, whilst those who find fault with it are a deluded lot who have lived in vain.

Giving up the fruits of action, free you will feel: There is no loss of effort, in this process nor a chance of incurring sin. Even the least bit of discipline saves you from retrogression and fear.

Establish yourself in this Yoga, take refuge in wisdom, be indifferent to both success and failure, perform your actions unattached, and tread the path of equanimity in Yoga that way.

A *Karma Yogi* in action may be seeing, hearing, speaking and doing such other acts in his daily life, but honestly he thinks in his state of pure realization that the real I in him is not the doer. Why so? Because, he knows that it is only when the sense-organs are in contact with the sense-objects that there is activity for the physical body, and that the seer in him is merely a witness—so he is not, in fact, the real doer.

So, mentally relegating all actions to the physical body, the city of nine gates, the self-controlled Yogi (already in Peace) now rests at ease in the Paradise of His Self, the *Brahma Puri* of his own Being—neither acting nor causing to act.

Dhananjaya! He is a Sage (Pandit) in whose case the desire for actions, action itself and even the very seed of thought are all consumed away in the fire of knowledge.

When one is rid of his desires in a state of renunciation of actions and relinquishment of possessions,* except those of bare necessity for his physical upkeep, (his thirst for enjoyment having died out), and when he is free from attachment to the objects and experiences around him, (as though unconcerned and indifferent), when his mind and sense organs remain unattached and well under control, *then* he attains the unique state of freedom from actions. And it is a state of freedom from actions and of the higher experience—of Naishkarma Siddhi.

A *Karma Yogi* (one integrated in actions) neither hates nor desires. He is as much a Sanyasi (renouncer) too, on that account free from the dual throngs of life go as well.

The Lord repeats: He who performs the ordained duties totally dedicating them to the Lord in veneration and identification without expectation of the fruits of action, is both a Yogi and Sanyasi (renouncer). He is not tainted by sin, just as the lotus by water. That is, he who has merely given up all his activities is no yogi, and likewise he who has merely renounced his sacred fire and other insignia is no Sanyase.

Finally, pursuing this path, it is the wiseman who sees inaction and action in inaction that is verily a Yogi who has accomplished all that he has to in his life.

---

*"Relinquishment of possessions" is not because such a person is driven to do it because of a proper understanding and revelation of the Truth in him, in which state he sees the emptiness of the ephemeral objects around him; and, the "immutability" of the soul within (the Atman).

Sacrificial Acts

The Lord says: Arjuna! Procedural details have been **laid down** in the scriptures (Vedas) for the performance of sacrificial **rites** (Yajnas) and these scriptures are the Ultimate (Sabda **Brahman**).

Scriptures relate to prescribed action (Karma). Sacrificial **acts** (Yajnas) relate to scriptures, to rains, food, and the created beings. And the all-pervading Brahman (Vedas) is said to be always present in sacrifice.

It is also said that, he who does not fall in line with this cycle of events but delights in the senses leads a life of sin, and he lives in vain.

After he created mankind together with this principle of sacrifice Brahma the Creator said:

Ye mankind shall properly perform these sacrificial acts (Yajnas). Let there be Kamadhenu, a source of fulfilment of your desires, for you.

Foster the gods and let the gods foster you too. Thus by fostering one another, you shall attain all that you want.

He who enjoys the fruits of the offerings alone (without partaking of it with the gods) is indeed a thief, and he who cooks food purely for himself, eats instead, the sins of his selfish deeds.

But virtuous people, on the other hand, who partake of what is left as a divine benediction (Prasad) are absolved of sins, and the yogins and the enlightened ones integrated in knowledge attain the eternal Brahman this way.

This very world we live in is said to be not a happy one without these virtues and humanitarian qualities and a spirit of service and sacrifice. How then the other?

The Lord says: Arjuna! The sacrificer, or the doer in you is Brahman. The act of oblation and the objects offered are Brahman: the sacrificial fire is also Brahman, and he who sees Brahman in all his actions as in the sacrificial act itself attains Brahman alone.

Some yogis perform sacrificial acts to propitiate the gods (*devas*). Some offer oblations to Brahman as the universal fire.

All perception through senses is sacrificed in the fire of self control. Even sensateness is allowed to be consumed away by the fire that resides within. . .

An offering of the sound and other objects of the sense-organs nto the respective upsurge of fire of self-control, an offering of the functions of all the organs and the vital breath (prana) into the fire of Yoga of an integrated Self (Atman) illumined by knowledge. Sacrificial acts with material objects, penance, gift, Yoga, austere vows, a study and understanding of the scriptures (Vedas), practice of the scriptural injunctions, are the other types of sacrificial acts that belong to the order of Yajna.

In this mode of Yajna and in the control of the vital force (Prana)[15] some offer the breath that is exhaled (Prana), into the one that is inhaled (apana), as also the incoming one into the outgoing. There are also others who restrain the very activity of breathing itself (Pranayama).

Some regulate and restrict their food, and offer as a sacrifice the functions of the Prana (vital breath), into that very force and source. All these pious men know the secret and the technique of sacrifice and sacrificial acts, and they are purified of their sins.

Arjuna! Many such acts of sacrifice have been stated in the scriptures (Vedas), but know them all as born of actions (Karma) only; and knowing thus, you will be free.

Worship of Gods

Partha! I abide equally in all and I am their source too. There is none hateful to me, or any dear. But those who devoutly worship Me abide in Me, and I also stand revealed to them.

Whatever may one approaches Me, even so I bless him. Whatever divine form one chooses to worship, I cause his faith to be unflinchingly attached to that one; and worshipping that way he too also obtains the objects of his desire which are granted by *Me* alone.

Those desiring quick results take to the worship of the gods (Devas) as the fruits of action follow quickly.

Certain others devoid of right understanding but swayed by passion, worship other deities as well—and for them the results are more transitory.

Surely, whilst My devotees attain Me only, those worshipping the gods reach the Gods, and the others worshipping the divinities gain their respective ends.

Am I not the enjoyer and the Lord of all sacrifices? So even those who worship the other gods worship Me alone, in truth though they do not know this or keep this fruit in their minds. The result is, they fail and falter, and do not reach the goal.

Certain spiritually advanced persons (Mahatmas) with austere vows and firm resolve remain steadfast in their minds and in their devotion to Me. Knowing Me as the imperishable, and as the prime cause they bow unto Me, derive happiness in constantly chanting My name in singing My glory, and in worshipping Me thus all the time.

Other virtuous men cleansed of their sins and freed from delusion worship Me with a firm resolve.

Again others of true knowledge (Jnana Yoga) betake them-selves to Me through their offering of knowledge (Jnana Yajna) and worship Me in My absolute aspect, as the One Lord in singleness (Ekatvam), or My omnipresent universal form in diverse ways, taking Me in diversity (visvatomukham).

Partha! Those who strive for freedom from decay and death, also take refuge in Me. They are the knowers, as well, of Brah-mam (*tat*), the infinite the entire field of action (karma) and the totality of the embodied Souls (Adhyatmam).

Adhyatmam, Adhibhutam

Krishna! What is that Brahmam? What is Adhyatmam? What is called Adhibutam and what is Adhideivam? Who, and how is the Adhiyajnam in this body known? How are you known by the self-restrained ones at the time of death?

The Lord says: Arjuna! The Supreme indestructible principle is Brahmam. This is also referred to as the unmanifest (avyak-tam). That is My abode, the Supreme goal, attaining which one does not return to this mortal world

One's own Self (Jeevatman) is Adhyatman: the offerings made with a spirit of sacrifice (Thyaga) and also those which cause the origin and development of beings is action (Karma).

The perishable entities are Adhibhutam. The cosmic being Brahman is Adhideivam And I, a witness (Sakshi) in this body is Adhiyajnan.

Partha! Those who know Me, together with what concerns the beings, the Gods, the sacrifices and My integral being, compris-ing of Adhibhutam (the field of matter) Adhideivam (Brahmam) and Adhiyajnam (the Unmanifest) and fix their minds on Me—they know Me even at the time of their death.

The Lord repeats. And he who remembers Me at the time of his death attains Me only. There is no doubt about it.

Dhananjaya, some ignorant people treat Me as any other human being only, and not knowing fully My supreme nature as the undecaying and unmanifest, deride Me.

But know that, even if a wicked person worships Me with sincere devotion; he has to be regarded as righteous only because he soon becomes righteous-minded, and striving for lasting peace, he attains it.

O SON OF KUNTI! MY DEVOTEE NEVER PERISHES . . . PROCLAIM THIS TO THE WORLD . . . .

Womenfolk, others in the Society of sinful birth, the low and the downtrodden—all of them verily reach the Supreme goal by taking refuge in Me.

What wonder then, that the holy and virtuous, and the devout royal Sages attain that too? Therefore, Arjuna, destined here, as you are, in this hapless world with fleeting experiences and no real happiness—with this, yes, even with this, and in this state of your life in this ephemeral world, worship Me.

Arjuna! Obsessed by desire, enamoured of the panegyric statements in the scriptural texts (Vedas), some dull witted persons indulge in flowery words and eulogize the various Vedic rites, holding heavens as the highest goal with nothing more higher and beyond.

These ones who are carried away by such words of flattery, and objects of sense pleasure fail to attain single-pointedness of mind and god realization.

The Vedas deal with the three modes of nature (Gunas); also speak about the means and ends of attaining worldly riches and pleasures. But be thou indifferent and unattached to them; and Ye shall also rise above the pairs of opposites.

Established ever thereafter in the eternal existence of Godhood, remaining totally unconcerned to the outer world phenomena and to the acquisition of worldly wealth and pleasures and to its preservation and protection thereof. This way thou shalt be redeemed, O Partha!

The Path of Knowledge

The Lord speaks: Arjuna! To you who are good-natured, I shall now impart the magnificent yoga of Knowledge (Jnana Yoga). It is excellent, enjoyable, attended with virtue, easy to practise, and established in this you will be free from evil.

So take refuge in Me; listen to this devoutly with your mind and being fixed on Me. You will then know Me in all my aspects. Resorting to this knowledge, the Sages were blessed with supreme felicity, and attaining My nature, they were not born again. But people lacking faith in all this do not reach Me: instead, they return to this mortal world only.

Partha! Know that the Lord does not accept the virtue or vice of anybody, that knowledge is enveloped by ignorance, that the pairs of opposites born out of aversion and desire, attraction and repulsion exist right from birth as yet another type of delusion. As for the world, it is also deluded by the three Gunas.

The Tripal aspects of Nature. Satva, Rajas and Tamas

Arjuna! There is nothing so sanctifying as knowledge. A blazing fire reduces its fuel to ashes. Even so the raging fire of knowledge reduces all actions, to nothingness.

In this integrated knowledge and Yoga, one actually experiences the revelation of the core of his being) in himself by himself.

O Son of Kunti! Know that all actions culminate in knowledge only, and that such a *Jnana Yajna*,[16] or the meditative type of offering of knowledge (at the feet of the Lord) is superior to the common sacrificial acts performed with material objects.

Knowledge and ignorance

Arjuna! Humility, unostentatiousness, non-violence, forgiveness, forbearance, uprightness, steadfastness, self-control, service to the preceptor (Guru)[17], purity of body and mind, dispassion for the sense objects, absence of egoism, realization of misery and an understanding of the inherent nature of the evils in birth and death, old age and sickness. . . absence of attachment whether good or evil befalls, unswerving devotion to Me, solitude, aversion for company, ceaseless enquiry into the fields of knowledge which reveals the Truth, and continuous efforts to revel in that revelation—all this is knowledge, which leads to immortality in the end. What is different from this is ignorance which leads to the perishable values.

O Son of Kunti! Attraction and repulsion are rooted in the sense-objects, and holding sway over them, the sense organs act as a stumbling block to knowledge. Sense-contacts are transitory and miserable, because they give rise to the opposites such as pain and pleasure, with a beginning and an end; and wisemen do not rejoice in them.

Brave Arjuna! Therefore ignore them, or endure them all. It is only such a person who remains unaffected and unruffled, and remains neither elated nor aggrieved, that is qualified for immortality

First control the sense-organs and the unsteady mind by the intellect; be steady and seated in knowledge; overcome the obstacles by defeating this hidden enemy difficult to conquer and which destroys realization . . . and now finally know the Self in you . . . realize the Atman which is beyond even the intellect and also the known and the unknown—That is your Asylum

Path of knowledge

Endowed with pure wisdom and understanding, controlling the body and mind with tenacity, restraining your speech, relinquishing the sense-objects, retreating to a sequestered place, eating *satvic* food, moderately laying aside your likes and dislikes, cultivating a sense of detachment and dispassion—*This way the Path of Knowledge (Jnana Yogam) has to be tread by you and the Truth realized.*

Forsaking egoism, power, arrogance, greed, desire, anger and the feeling of meum, and finally remaining calm and composed after all this quest—*Now, in this state you are in actual experience of the Eternal Brahmam.*

Arjuna says: Lord! You seem to confuse me. If the path of knowledge is superior to the path of action, then why direct me to this dreadful course? Please tell me that which is of the greatest good.

The Lord replies: O Sinless one! Originally a two-fold path was declared by me—the path of Knowledge for the Sankhyas and the path of action for the Karma Yogis.

Here, in regard to actions, a true relinquisher is one who has relinquished the fruits of action; so, he is a hypocrite who only outwardly restrains the sense organs, but inwardly sits mentally on the sense objects. In the same way, an unattached person who takes up the performance of actions (Yoga of actions) in physical and mental self-control excels. Not the others

Continuing the Lord says: This path of knowledge is so secure that, even if you happen to be the worst sinner amongst all sinners, yet you will be able to cross all sins by this raft of knowledge.

And, in the case of those enlightened people whose ignorance has been dispelled by knowledge, The Light of the Self, this illumination reveals the Supreme, as the Sun does the objects of the world outside.

Surrender to your spiritual mentor and seek this knowledge further with humility, a guileless heart, and an enquiring and a spirit of service. The wise Mahatmas who are knowers of Truth will guide you in the path.

Arjuna! Some meditate on the Self (Atman) in their own hearts, and some others do so in a state of silent introspection.[18] There are also others who take up to the Path of Knowledge and the Path of Action, towards the same goal of self-realization.[19]

Partha! The Mahatmas in self realization whose mind and intellect are totally merged in the Supreme, who are devoted to that. Ultimate being, and who take refuge in that last resort, attain a state of no return to this mortal world, as all their sins have been winnowed off by knowledge.

And to such a great Soul[20] with an equanimity of mind and the constant awareness in which the supreme self, is experienced the same as in the other beings, as well as in himself—to him a Brahmin, a cow, an elephant, a dog and an outcaste are all equals.

Such ones established in faith, zeal, self-control and devotion to this Supreme goal soon attain true knowledge and transcendental peace; and getting over the dual throngs of life, they remain unshaken with no easy slipover or stepdown.

The serene self-controlled persons who are alike to the dual experiences of life remain well established in the Path of Knowledge but there are others who may not understand this Truth at the highest level, but are, all the same, sincere at heart. Their way of worship lies in the constant hearing of the Truth from others (Sravanam). Verily they too go beyond death.[21]

Dhananjaya! Purified by their knowledge and penance, freed from passion, fear and anger, many have attained Me, with their minds intent on Me in total identification and surrender.

But as for the man wanting in faith and lingering in doubt, there is neither this, nor the other world. There is no happiness for him either: he heads only for his ruination.

Therefore, O Descendant of Bharata. . . arise.

With the sword of knowledge, cut asunder the doubts in your mind born of ignorance, and in the resultant enlightened mood, take to Yoga,[22] the art of integration.

Continuing the Lord says: Arjuna! Men of wisdom grieve not for those who should not be grieved for; nor do they sorrow over the dead or the living.

Balanced in mind and established in that eternal state (Brahman) they neither rejoice on getting what is pleasant, nor grieve on facing what is unpleasant. Undeluded, alike to all beings, they are supreme in their devotion to Me.

This way, they know Me and My reality—Who I am. . What I am . . . What My glory is. Crossing the frontiers of life and knowledge, they become one with Me and attain Me only. This is the consummation of the Yoga of knowledge.

The absolute Brahmam is free from blemish.[23] It is equanimous ever. And attaining an equanimity of mind and getting established in Brahmam, the pious Yogins conquer birth this way here itself, instantly.

Repeating it, men of wisdom (Sages) and others in renunciation and self-realization with their doubts dispelled, free from sin, passion and anger, and devoted to the welfare of all beings, get absorbed (liberated) in Brahmam here and hereafter.

Such wise persons illumined by the Light of Lights (Atman) are a happy lot delighting in the Self (Atman) within—and they reach the frontiers of knowledge and attain liberation in Brahmam, here itself, even while alive. (It is fantastic, but all real and comforting to the tortured Soul.)

Arjuna! Know that one whose mind is not drawn towards the external sense-objects experiences the bliss of his own Self (Atmanubhavam), and again the same person, when he is totally identified *introspectively* with the Supreme Brahman, enjoys undecaying Bliss.[24]

Partha! When one intuitively perceives the diversified existence of the beings as rooted in his own Self (Atman), and likewise their emergence from his own Self (Atman)—then, that very moment there is realization of *Truth* in him, and he becomes *Brahmam* himself.

He who experiences the Supreme Lord abiding equally in all beings, as in himself, and also identifies Him as the only imperishable substance among the perishables—He is the right seer who sees light and sees right!

And (most important of all) in this process he does not also bring about his own self-effacement. On the other hand, he uplifts himself, and fulfils the mission of his life.

Dhananjaya! All this is a rare happening, because among thousands, one per chance takes up this course of spirituality, self analysis and self-realization; rarer still is one who is again nearer perfection, and even amongst those that are perfect, one, per chance, knows Me in Truth.

One of steady wisdom (Sthitha Prajnan)

Arjuna enquires of the Lord: O Keshava! What are the characteristics of a Sthitha Prajnan—a person of steady wisdom rooted in contemplation (self-realization and Samadhi)? How does he move about and live in this world?

The Lord clarifies: Arjuna! He who has his sense-organs under control, remains in a composed state and devotes himself heart and Soul to Me has indeed established himself in knowledge (Prajna).

One is said to be a Mahatman or a Sage when he is steady in

his knowledge is free from fear, anger and desire remains unperturbed and unconcerned about joy and sorrow and the dual throngs of life, who neither welcomes nor rejects what comes his way, who feels neither elated when things go better, nor feels sorrowful when they go wrong, and who, all the time, remains unattached to everything around him—(not helplessly, but out of conviction).

When one completely shuns the cravings of his mind, but rejoices in the Truth of his real Self (Atman), and the infinitude of his own being (Atman), then he is said to be established in true knowledge.

Arjuna! A person of steady wisdom (Sthitha Prajnan) is able to completely withdraw his sense-organs from the sense-objects, even as a tortoise does, with ease, when it wants to.

Note that the food[25] or the sense-objects cease to be for one who has abandoned his likings therefore except his relish or the taste.

But even this relish drops off when he is in commune with the Supreme Reality.

Is it not that the sense-organs which are turbulent by nature, forcibly draw away the minds of even the steady (and sturdy too) seekers from their pursuits?

The Lord says: He who thinks of, and broods over the sense-objects, derives an attachment for them.

The further process is this: from attachment is born desire, from desire ensues anger, from anger results infatuation, from infatuation to lapse of memory, from lapse of memory to loss of reason and understanding, and from loss of reason and the resultant destruction of one's own intelligence, (Buddhi Nasam) there is ruination for him—the end.

So placidity of mind is a divine boon for one who is tranquil, self-controlled and well-settled in the path of spirituality. For him, his sorrows and miseries come to an end (in this life itself) even though he may be in action and in enjoyment of the object of this world—(of course, if only he has learnt to be free[26] from attachment thereto or aversion therefore.

On the other hand there is neither peace nor happiness for one whose mind is unsettled, who lacks right understanding, correct knowledge (viveka), and proper reasoning, and has not also the capacity for introspection and meditation. How can there be happiness for one wanting peace of mind?

As the wind does a barge upon waters, even so a wandering mind does, and whichever sense-organ it follows, that way it draws one's discrimination as well. Therefore it is that one who is able to restrain his mind and the sense-organs that is well established in knowledge.

To such a Sage (Muni)[27] in the ecstacy of self-realization and Truth, that which is night to all beings, is one of day, and '*that*' which is day, night.

One established in knowledge (Sthitha Prajna) remains ever unruffled. Even though different rivers join the ocean, which though full already, remains the same even after the big confluence, so is the state of one of true knowledge in whom there is no uprising, overflow, or dearth in the experience of Truth and in whom all desires have merged and consummated.

The Lord says: Arjuna! He who is rid of his ego and the attachment to the sense-objects, but who moves about detached from the world, and devoid of any thoughts of "me" and "mine" alone attains Peace.

Remaining in this state even if it be at the time of his death,[28] the Yogi attains the Brahmic Bliss, the highest ever undeluded and undiluted one.

What is that Brahmam?

The Lord says: Arjuna! I will now tell you about that, upon knowing which one transcends the frontiers of death and attains immortality. It is the supreme Brahmam without a beginning, which is neither a being nor a state of existence (sat) as such, nor a non-being or non-existence (asat) for that matter.

With its ears, hands and feet everywhere, with its head and face likewise everywhere, it rests pervading the entire world.

Though devoid of sense-organs, it is manifest in their functions; though unattached and without attributes, it sustains everything, and remains also as the upholder and protector of the virtuous qualities (nay, all qualities).

It is within and without: it is moving and yet unmoving: it is far, yet near, and by reason of its subtlety, it is incomprehensible.

It is undivided, yet remains as if divided. That "knowable" being is the sustainer of all beings (Vishnu), destroyer (Rudra), and creator (Brahma)

This Light of Lights which is beyond all darkness is the Atman abiding in the hearts of all beings. It is the knowledge, the knowable and the one to be realized through pure knowledge.

Knowing this, My devotee attains Me and the State of My being—*so says the Lord.*

OM TAT SAT:[29] This is a three-way sound symbol indicative of Brahmam. By that, of old, the Brahmins, the Vedas and the sacrifices were formulated.

With the monosyllable *OM* acts of sacrifice, gift and penance are commenced well; and with the belief that everything belongs to Him, the ultimate Being—*Tat*—true seekers of liberation perform such acts without expectation of the fruits of such actions.

And *Sat* is used to denote existence and goodness, and also in relation to auspicious and praiseworthy acts.

Arjuna! Steadfastness in performance of penance and sacrifice, and interestedness in offering gifts are *Sat*—also acts incidental thereto (and dedicated to the Lord) are that.

Those, and other holy and humanitarian acts done without faith are termed *asat*. They are nought here and hereafter.

Prakriti and Yoga

The Lord says: Arjuna! There are two types of men in this world—the Divine and the demoniacal. Divine virtues are conducive to liberation and the demoniacal ones to bondage. And you are born with Divine virtues only.

The Divine virtues are: fearlessnes, pure heart, charity, austerity, self control, steadfastness of mind, absorption in knowledge and Yoga, performance of sacrificial acts (Yajnas) uprightness and a study of the scriptures:

Non-violence in thought, word and deed, truthfulness, absence of anger, absence of fickleness, abstention from slander, non-covetousness, modesty, tranquillity of mind, gentleness, kindness to all beings, and a sense of detachment, in a spirit of sacrifice. . . boldness, cleanliness, fortitude, forgiveness, absence of conceit and malice. . .

The demoniacal qualities are: ostentation, arrogance, pride, anger, harshness, ignorance and delusion.

Men of demoniac nature are neither pure, nor good, nor truthful, and they know not what is right activity and what is right cessation of activity.

They go about saying "This world is full of untruth, without a God, and all that we see around is the outcome of lust, of the union of men and women. What else could there be?

Holding such base and barren views on life, they are the sworn enemies born for their own destruction. With hypocrisy, pride, arrogance and delusion they resort to endless actions with unholy intentions only for the fulfilment of their insatiable desires.

Lost in endless cares and worries which end only with death, and given to the enjoyment of sensuous objects, they go about saying. . . . It is this . . . and this way only and Enjoyment is the essence of life. Given to lust and anger, and bound by the innumerable ties of life these people (naturally) strive to amass wealth by means fair or foul.

They also go about always inmersed in such thoughts as: I have had this gain today, and more of my desires will be shortly fulfilled. This wealth is mine already, and I will acquire a greater lot soon. . . . This enemy has been slain, and others too I will destroy. I am the Lord. I am happy, successful and I powerful, and I am having all the enjoyments of life.

· I am rich, and of noble birth too. I will rejoice. Who else is equal to me? I will perform sacrifices, offer gifts . . .

Filled with vanity, and the haughtiness of their wealth, they perform sacrifices only in name, ostentatiously and contrary to prescribed procedures.

Possessed of power, insolence, lust, ego and anger, they cavil at Me—hating Me, that dwelleth in their own bodies and in those of others. They envy, too, the pious and good-natured.

Deluded by ignorance, perplexed by fantasy, addicted to sensuous pleasures, such people of a demoniac nature fall into foul hell and they are consigned by Me to the world of transmigratory existence.

Arjuna! Those with vain hopes, futile actions, fiendish nature and fruitless knowledge, who practise austerities not enjoined by the scriptures, and in this process torment themselves and Me

too, the dweller in the body (hearts), those given to ostentation, self-conceit, egoism, attachment, desire and the pride of
power—Know them all to be of demoniac resolve.

Alas! Birth after birth these deluded people go from bad to
worse without ever seeking to attain Me.

Passion, anger and greed are the triple Gateways to Hell,
and to destruction of one's own being (Self). They are to be
shunned.

An aspirant (Sadhak) released from these evil forces practises
what is good for his liberation and reaches the highest goal,
whereas one who acts in gay abandon casting aside the injunctions of the scriptures attains neither peace nor perfection, nor
happiness nor the supreme goal.

Dhananjaya! So let the scriptures be your authority in determining what ought to be done and what ought not to be done,
and then you follow the prescribed course and take the permis-
sive line of actions to reach your goal.

The triple aspects of nature

The Lord continues: There is nothing on earth, or in the
heavens which is free from the triple nature—Satvam, Rajas and
Tamas: and I will now tell you all about these which encumber
the embodied Souls.

Satvic quality is the result of virtuous actions: it is immaculate,
luminous and flawless, and binds an individual by its attachment
to knowledge and happiness.

So, whenever you experience the Light of Knowledge, then
indeed know that Satvam is predominant: and, with this quality
predominating at the time of death, one attains the higher
worlds.

Rajas is of the nature of passion, desire and attachment. Greed, grief, initiative for actions, activity itself, restlessness and pain are the results of Rajoguna which binds the embodied Soul with its effects.

If Rajoguna is uppermost at the time of death the person is reborn in this world amongst those attached to work.

Tamas is born of ignorance, and it binds the Soul through delusion, slovenliness, sloth and sleep; obtuseness, inactivity, carelessness and stupor are the effects of Tamo guna.

When a man of Tamoguna dies he goes down to the lower realms of life and is reborn in the family of irrational beings.

Know that Satvam prevails suppressing Rajas and Tamas. Rajas suppresses Satvam and Tamas, and Tamas, when predominant, suppresses both Satvam and Rajas.

Arjuna! When the pure discriminating intellect, the seer, in its wisdom and experience beholds no other active agent than the three Gunas, and the seer is also further aware of that which is beyond the triple aspects of nature, that is Me, then he attains immortality—freedom from birth, death, old age and misery.

Arjuna asks: Lord! What are the characteristics of one who has transcended the three Gunas described by you?

The Lord says: Arjuna! The three Gunas are inseparably there with everyone, as knowledge (Satvam), activity (Rajasam), and delusion (Tamasam) . . .

He who is established in the blissful experience of his own Self (Atman), who is calm and composed, alike to both joy and sorrow, censure and praise, honour and dishonour, friend and

foe, pleasant and unpleasant things, . . . who remains as though
indifferent to the outer world manifestations has neither aversion
nor an aspiration, has renounced his agency for actions, and also
his desire for the fruits of same, to whom a clod of earth, a
stone and goal is of equal worth, who is aware that he as the
higher Self as a mere dispassionate witness to the play of the
Gunas, and that the Gunas alone are the basic cause for such
activities i.e. they alone act, such a person without a wavering
and a wandering mind remains steady and unshaken: and he is
said to have transcended the Gunas.

Faith, food and worship

Arjuna enquires of the Lord further. Lord! One is endowed
with Faith* but he casts aside the scriptural injunctions. What
is his status? It is Satvic, Rajasic or Tamasic?

The Lord replies: Arjuna! Faith or fidelity born of conviction
(Sraddha), is of three kinds—Satvic, Rajasic and Tamasic.

Faith is the very essence of man, and one is verily what his
faith is.

Men of Satvic disposition worship the Gods, those of Rajas
worship the Yaksha and Rakshas as and Tamasic people worship
the spirits and ghosts.

Classifying food—it is of three kinds. Food which promotes
longevity and gives energy, strength, health, happiness and joy,
and which is sweet, bland, nourishing and agreeable, is of the
Satvic variety.

The Rajoguna variety is food which is bitter, sour, saltish,
hot, pungent, dry and irritating and productive of pain, grief
and disease.

Tamasic food is half-cooked, insipid, putrid, stale, polluted

---

*Faith (Shraddha) is not here mere 'belief' as the word would mean.
Instead, it is interestedness or sheer earnestness in the performance of
actions, or doing our duty or any undertaking, for that matter.

(partly eaten by others) and also impure.

Performance of sacrifical acts according to the scriptural injunctions with no desire for the fruits of action, but with the firm belief that it is all duty performed is Satvic.

Those performed with the expectation for the fruits of action and in an ostentatious manner are all Rajasic.

Tamasic sacrificial acts are those lacking earnestness and faith, which have no sanction of the scriptures, in which no food is distributed, no sacred formula followed, and no mantras chanted, with no gifts to the priests and those assembled.

Satvic austerities are those done with supreme faith with no desire for the fruits of action.

These Satvic ones are also of three types. Physical austerity is worship of the Gods, the Brahmins (*i.e.* men of true learning and self realization), the preceptor, the wise, and also purity, fair-mindedness, continence and non-violence.

Unoffensive wholesome talk which is truthful and pleasant, as also a study of the Vedas (the sacred scriptures) are the Satvic type of austerity of speech.

Satvic mental austerity is serenity of mind, kindliness, silence, self-control and purity of heart and outlook.

Rajasic type of austerity is practised with ostentation and show with the object of winning respect, honour and adoration and it is transitory and unstable.

Austerity practised with possible self-torture or with a stubborn idea to cause injury to others, is of the Tamasic type.

"It is my duty to give"—an offering (Dana) is of the Satvic type if it is made with this firm belief to one who has *not* helped in the past, or whom we do not expect to reciprocate in future.

Further, such a gift should pleasingly be given with due regard to proper place, time and the recipient thereof, for its worthiness in every way.

What is given grudgingly with a reciprocal intantion or arrangement, or with an eye on a gain or profit, is of the Rajasic type.

A gift given away at an inappropriate time and place to an unworthy person with disdain and disrespect is Tamasic.

Relinquishment: Actions enjoined by the scriptures, and done as duty only giving up the attachment thereto and relinquishing the fruits or action—that type of relinquishment is satvic.

A relinquisher, satvic by nature, discriminating and steady in his understanding with his doubts dispelled, desires not, desists not even other actions than those of sacrifice, gift or penance.

If, out of fear of sustaining any physical trouble, actions are relinquished as irksome, than it is the Rajasic type, and the fruits of relinquishment are lost.

It is incompatible to renounce certain basic ordained duties (obligatory ones) prescribed by the scriptures, because they have necessarily to be performed. Their abandonment or non-performance through ignorance is said to be Tamasic.

Arjuna, knowledge, action and the doer are of three kinds according to Gunas.

Satvic *knowledge* is that by which one understands the one undivided imperishable being as the one undivided only, among the divided beings and existence of this world.

The one Self (Atman) resides in the hearts of all: *but* he who regards as separate and manifold only the various existence on earth, is of the Rajasic type in his knowledge.

The knowledge which is trivial, irrational, contrary to Truth, and which hangs on tenaciously to this limited body and pertinaciously believes this unit to be the whole (Atman) is of the Tamasic variety.

Satvic *action* is the ordained duty performed without attachment, passion and prejudice, and *not* seeking the fruits of action.

One possessed of ego and prompted by desire and resorting to actions involving much trouble, solely for the sake of enjoyment of pleasure is of the Rajasic type.

Actions undertaken through delusion without due regard to consequences, one's own capacity, possible loss to oneself, and inconvenience or injury to others are Tamasic.

A Satvic doer is free from attachment, non-egoistic, endowed with fortitude and vigour, and unaffected by success or failure.

A Rajasic doer is one of impure conduct, violent, greedy, passionate and desirous of the fruits of action and subject to elation and dejection.

A Tamasic doer lacks self-control and piety, is of unsteady mind, vulgar, arrogant, slothful, deceitful, despondent, inclined to rob others of their livelihood, and of a procrasting type.

Arjuna! The faculty of mind has a three-fold division according to the Gunas (nature), of reason* and of tenacity. They are: The faculty of mind which knows the art and the act of engagement in and disengagement from actions, what ought to be done and ought not to be done, knows fear and absence of fear, and bondage and liberation, is of the Satvic type.

The Rajasic type is that which understands incorrectly the right and the wrong and the do's and don'ts of actions, taking them differently from what they are.

The faculty of mind (Buddhi) which in ignorance interprets

*Here reason is to be taken as the mental faculty, to draw the pros and cons and conclusions, and determine what is right and what is wrong, and what is truth and untruth.

unrighteouness as righteousness only, and looks at the objects of the world in a perverse way is Tamasic.

The tenacity which is unswerving in and through Yoga, and by which one is able to control the mind, the sense-organs and the life-breaths (prana) is Satvic.

The Rajasic type is that by which a person holds fast to the first three only of the four prime stands of life (Pursharthas) viz. virtue (Dharma) wealth (Artha) and pleasure (Kama)—the foruth, liberation (Moksha), not being in his list or concern.

Tamasic tenacity is that by which a stupid person does not abandon sleep, fear, grief, despondency and pride.

The happiness which one attains in the practice of prayer, meditation and worship, whereby one comes to the end of his sorrows and mental disquiettude, that which is seemingly unpleasant in the beginning, but sweet and nectar-like at the end—that placidity of mind and serenity of understanding born of the Light of his own Self is of the Satvic type of happiness.

The happiness which arises from a contact with the sense objects, and which appears to be pleasant in the beginning, but turns out to be injurious and harmful in the end, is of the Rajasic type.

The Tamasic type of happiness is what is delusory and deadening both at the beginning and end, and which arises from sleep, lassitude and carelessness.

The art of integration—Yoga

The Lord says: Arjuna! Originally I imparted this science to Vivasvan, and he, in turn to Manu, and Manu passed it on to Ikshvahu.

This Yoga known to such *rajarshis* has since become extinct due to efflux of time, and now to you, my devotee and friend, I pass on this science.

Arjuna in doubt asks the Lord: Lord! Your birth was much later than that of Vivasvan. How is it then that you taught this science to him in the beginning?

The Lord says: Arjuna! You and I have passed through many births: I know them all, while you don't. In fact, there was never a time when I was not, nor these kings, nor that we shall not exist hereafter.

Partha! When your confused mind with its conflicting stand turns inwards and remains steadfastly and introspectively in the Self (Atman), when it is free from its desires and cravings for enjoyments, actions, and to the sense-objects as well, know then, you have attained the state of Yoga. Set yourself to this Yoga, take refuge in wisdom, perform your actions unattached, be indifferent to both success and failure, and this way you tread the path of equanimity in Yoga.

Yoga is dexterity in action. Be thou endowed with it at all times.

In the enlightened state in which the mind crosses the mire of delusion, there arises a right kind of apathy in regard to what has already been heard and what is more to be heard and read—the acquisition of knowledge loses its importance.

·To the karma yogi (who seeks perfection through action) action is said to be the means and his accomplishment in that technique of cessation from actions is his success at that level with the resultant tranquillity of mind his blessedness.

Renunciation of actions and integration in actions

Arjuna! That which is extolled as Sanyas (renunciation of actions) is Yoga too: and no one becomes a Yogi so long as he has his desires and the expectation of the fruits of actions and the latent intentions (Sankalpas) which are the root cause for all actions. So without Yoga one does not attain the peace inherent in renunciation.

Whilst the harmonized person well established in Yoga attains the state of *sanyas* too, and eventually the status of *Brahman*, the Supreme, the non-harmonized one (swayed by passion, desire and attachment) is committed to bondage.

Renunciation and relinquishment

Arjuna says: Lord! I desire to know the true nature of renunciation (Sanyas) and also of that of relinquishment (Thyaga).

The Lord answers: Some wisemen consider the very renunciation of actions prompted by desire as Sanyas, whilst others define relinquishment of the fruits of all actions (Thyaga) as good as sanyas. Some others opine that all actions are to be treated as evil, and should be abandoned. There are others still who say that acts of sacrifice, gift and penance should not be given up, but indeed, they should be befittingly done; giving up the attachment and the desire for the fruits thereof because they purify the pious ones in their spiritual pursuit.

Arjuna! It is the ignorant, ones who say that knowledge (Sankhya) and Yoga are different. It is not so, because, the very status which is attained by men of knowledge is also attained by men of selfless action. So practising even one, thoroughly, a person attains the fruits of both.

Yoga

The well-settled state in which the mind becomes unwearied, and rests at ease, in which the pure intellect visualizes the Self (Atman) within and introspectively rejoices; established in which one does not stray from Truth, or consider any other acquisition to be of greater value—that state free from a combination and an admixture of evil, pain and sorrow inherent in the objects of the world, when in contact with is a priceless acquisition. It is the Yoga of eternal worth, and of everlasting virtue which merits earnest practice with a firm resolve, conviction and an unswerving mind.[29]

Renouncing his desires and resorting to a clean and secluded place, remaining fearless on a seat neither too high nor too low, of Kusha grass, deer skin, and a cloth spread ont op, with the body and head erect, with the sense organs and mind well under control, pledged to continence, gazing at the tip of the nose for single-pointedness, not looking around, not thinking of anything else, but tranquil in mind, with thoughts on *Me* as the Supreme goal, thus should one practice Yoga for self-purification.

Arjuna! Eating too much, or sleeping too long, or not eating at all, or being ceaselessly awake—these are the obstacles to Yoga.

But Yoga which wards off unhappiness in the wake of the awakening it creates, is easy to attain by one who is moderate in these, and in his other daily avocations.

Arjuna says in retrospect: Lord! A turbulent mind restless in its nature is difficult to control, like the wind; because of this I have not been able to grasp what you say about the efficacy of Yoga.

The Lord's reply: Arjuna! Surely it is difficult to control a restless mind, but by practice and firm resolve, you can restrain it and successfully wean it away from the sense-objects and turn it inwards, in quest of self-realization.

And in this regard, one's own Self is his friend or foe. So, all the time one should be alert and uplift himself by his own efforts and not degrade himself.

So he is a friend unto himself who has conquered the Self (body and mind) by his own Self (enlightenment and intellect) but for the uncontrolled one, however, he alone confronts himself as though he is an enemy unto himself.

Arjuna in doubt asks the Lord again: Lord! Though endowed

with faith, one strives not in his path. Unable to subdue his mind, he is diverted from Yoga and he does not attain perfection. What happens to him then? Does he perish like a torn cloud, deprived both of God realization and worldly enjoyments or what?

The Lord answers: Neither here, nor hereafter there' is any destruction for such a person, because the doer of good never comes to evil.

What happens is this: having attained the higher worlds to which men of meritorious deeds go, and residing there for a pretty long time, he is born again in the families of either the pious or wealthy ones.

Or, he may be born in the family of the enlightened Yogis, but this kind of birth is rare indeed. Here, unaware of it himself, he intuitively picks up the latent threads of Yoga and the even-mindedness of his previous births, and continues to strive for greater perfection than before.

One is drawn, away from or nearer, to God realization by such unseen influences of his pre-natal habits and practices, and he who strives sincerely in this path, even as a mere enquirer, transcends the binding effects of actions (Karma) in course of time.

In the case of a Yogi, however, who practises assiduously, and is purified of his sins, he attains the highest goal after passing through many births (with the helpful features of a progressive type of acquired tendencies, latencies and legacies of his previous births—Vasanas).

In short, a Yogi is greater than ascetics, greater than even men of knowledge, and greater also than those devoted to work. Therefore, be a Yogi, O Arjuna!

My opinion is, of all Yogis he who devoutly worships Me with faith and with his mind absorbed in Me, is the best—concludes the Lord.

Yogis and their experience

The Lord says: When one is rid of desires, is bereft of attachment to the sense-objects and sense-organs, is free from the
cravings for enjoyment, when his mind in self-control rests easily
on the Self (Atman)—then such a one with a spirit of renunciation too, is said to have attained Yoga.

And he who is able to withstand in this very life before his
death the regular onslaughts of his mind arising out of passion
and anger, and establish himself very well in his spirits (Atman)
without any depression is a happy one indeed.

Arjuna! By his own intellect and gradual practice one should
shift his mind on to the Self, constantly regulated by concentration and steadfastness. Such a Yogi integrated in his mind and
equanimous in his view identifies himself with the outer beings
around him on the analogy of his own Self. Because he sees the
Self of his own Being (Atman) in all beings, and all beings
equally in his own Self (Atman). Such a Yogi is truly great.

The Lord says: Partha! He who sees Me everywhere and sees,
also all things in Me . . . such a person does not lose sight
of Me, nor do I, of him. I am easily accessible to those ever
restrained Yogis.

That Yogi dwells in Me alone, who, whatever his way of life
and actions, divested of his difference and dualities rests blis-
sfully in that one reality which is equally present in all beings,
he thereby worships Me with an awareness and an experience
of His Self (Atman) remaining all the time in that unique state.

Arjuna! Even as a lamp sheltered from the wind does not
flutter, so too a Yogi in self control meditating on God does not
falter: he remains calm.

Washed of the evils of Rajoguna, contented, single-minded,
resting in the Peace of of his heart, the Bliss of his Self, the
infinitude of his existence he is in commune with. . .

Because of all these subtle, inward contact experience with Brahmam (Brahma Samsparam), he revels in that Supreme Brahmananda only, and remains totally identified with that very infinitude, the eternal Peace that I am (and He is and You are), so says the Lord.

Such a spiritually advanced person with an equanimity of mind excels—one who is alike to everyone to a well wisher, a friend, a foe, a neutral, an arbiter, a person hated or one who hates, a relation, one virtuous and one sinful too. . . and to him in knowledge and experience (Yoga) a clod of earth, a stone and gold are all of equal worth.

It is by constant practice of meditation and contemplation that the Yogis attain, when in a settled introspective mood, the status of the Supreme Lord of the *Parama Purusha*, and the *Param Sthanam.*

He who, at the time of his death (at least then) meditates upon Him, fixing his life-breath between the eye brows, as in Yoga, even that person attains Him.

He who knows ME as the great Lord of the worlds, the enjoyer of the sacred offerings made and austerities performed, and as the well-wisher of all beings—he too attains that peace and liberation.

This Supreme Being, the one who is resplendent like the Sun is described as the all knowing, the ancient, the ruler of all, subtler than the subtlest, the sustainer of all, bestower of the fruits of actions, beyond comprehension and of the darkness of ignorance too, and yet the one coginsable in the light of His illumination.

The Lord says: Arjuna I shall now tell you about the Supreme goal which the knowers of Vedas proclaim as the Imperishable one, (aksharam) and desiring which those in celibacy and renunciation resort to.

First restraining the media of perception then withdrawing the mind from the head where it is ever active; next, seating it in the heart in its silence, controlling the life-breath, and holding it on in a state of meditation and concentration at the subtle summit spot in the head (Moordha) to enable it to delve deep and dissolve itself, and finally holding a firm ground on integration and union with the Lord within, in Yoga—he who casts off his mortal coil in this manner with his mind set on Me alone in that silence, and reciting the sacred mono-syllable *Om*—such a spiritually advanced person (Soul) attains the highest goal.

Upon death there is a twofold path for men. Whilst the Yogi reaches the Supreme State from which there is no return by the one, the others who have taken up to the path of action return to mortal world by the other.

In one is evident the all-effulgent fire god, the gods presiding over daytime, the bright fortnight (Sukla paksha) the six months of the northern solstice (Uttarayanam)—a path of no return, eventually.

In the other is manifest the gods presiding over smoke or darkness, night, the dark fortnight (Krishna paksha) and the six months *of* the southern solstice (Dakshinayanam)—come back for them to this mortal world.

O Son of Kunti! An accomplished Yogi transcends everything that is glorified for those that study the scriptures (Vedas) perform austerities, and offer charities, because he finally attains the eternal Brahmam (Param Sthanam).

Partha! All the worlds including that of Brahma the creator are subject to recurrence, but for those who attain Brahmam, there is no such happening as thus they reach Me.

So thinking of whatever object one leaves his body at the

time of death* he attains that very status.

Arjuna so thinking of Me alone, with your mind and intellect totally on Me in devotion and dedication you shall attain Me. There is no doubt about it.

In the case of all such pious ones devoted to Me, I concern Myself with their welfare and prosperity assuring them in all respects.

Arjuna! Some persons versed in the scriptures (Vedas) worship Me, aspiring for celestial pleasures, but heaven is not an eternal place for infinite enjoyment, because they are attained by finite actions only; so those learned scholars return to this world of mortality when the period of their stay and enjoyment is over.

Good, bad and mixed are the threefold fruits of action for such men who repeatedly tread this path, to and from heavens, but for those who have renounced them all, there is none ever like that.

*Generally one is haunted at the time of his death by that thought which had engaged his mind most during his life time. As a rule, therefore, it is this predominating thought which determines his future course.

The Gateway to Heaven

The Lord says: Arjuna! Fix your mind on Me in devotion and overcome all obstacles through My grace. If, however, you do not listen to me in self-conceit, and prompted by ego you should still say "I will not fight," then it is a vain resolve, because "the nature in you" will ultimately prevail to compel you to do what, you now do not wish to do out of delusion (Moha).

Partha! Considering your own duty you ought not to waver, or grieve because for a *Kshatriya*-warrior like you, there is nothing more glorious than a righteous battle—and here is one for you.

Happy are those of this clan who die fighting in a righteous battle, because *that* is said to be a Gateway to Heaven. So if you do not fight this righteous battle then you will fail in your duty, lose your reputation, get degraded, and incur sin. Your enemies will think you have withdrawn from the battlefield in fear and talk disparagingly about your might and eternal infamy; and for one like you, held in high esteem, this disgrace is worse than death. What can be more cruel and disturbing than this?

Either killed in battle you attain heaven, or gaining victory you enjoy the sovereignty of the earth. Therefore arise Arjuna!

Mentally surrender all actions to *Me* regard *Me* as the Supreme goal, and resort to the Yoga of Equanimity, constantly fixing your mind on Me.

Treating alike pleasure and pain, gain and loss, victory and defeat, get ready for the fight; and, fighting thus, you incur no sin.

The all-powerful Lord is enshrined in the hearts of all beings, with his Maya Sakti, (mystic macrocosmic power deluding in its nature), and *He* ordains the course of all beings by the inexorable Law of Nature.[30]

O Descendent of Bharata! Take refuge in Him with all your heart; by His grace you shall attain supreme peace and the eternal abode.

Disown the agency for actions and the fruits thereof.

Give up all duties in that sense. Take refuge in *Me*, and I will liberate you from all Sins—Do not grieve.*

Now reflect fully and act as you like

Arjuna! As you are dear to Me, hear again My Supreme word! On Me, fix thy mind. To Me, bring thy devotion.

To Me, offer thy sacrifice: To Me, indeed, shalt thou come. Solemn is My promise to Thee, for, thou are dear to Me.

Partha! Have you listened with undivided attention to what all I have said? Are you rid of the ignorance born out of delusion?

Arjuna says: Lord! My delusion is gone. I have re-gained true knowledge through Your grace . . . and it has re-established (stabilized) my memory and the right power of understanding as well.

Rid of my doubts, therefore, I will carry out your biddings.

Arjuna! This teaching should not be imparted to one who has no austerity and devotion, nor to one unwilling to hear, and also

---

*Arjuna is not forced to accept what the Lord has said, because the choice has been left entirely to Arjuna himself. The teachings of the Lord come to an end with this sloka, but as though out of compassion and in retrospect, *He* benignly continues.

not to one who cavils at Me. Instead, he who passes this on to My sincere devotees serves Me well. There is none on earth, who is more dearer to Me, than he and he attains Me alone in the end.

In my opinion, even he who merely studies this sacred dialogue between us with fervour is one who worships Me through *Jnana Yajna.**

Even a person who only hears this from others, with devotion is freed from turmoil and bondage, and he attains the highest state of existence usually attained by men of righteous conduct.

Sanjaya's joy

Sanjaya says to Dhritarashtra. Thus have I heard personally, through the grace of Sage Vyasa, this wonderful dialogue between Yogeswara Krishna and Partha.

O King Dhritarashtra! I rejoice ceaselessly, and great indeed is my wonder whenever I recall to my mind this soul-stirring conversation as also the resplendent form of Sri Hari.

Wherever Sri Krishna, the Lord of Yoga is and Wherever is Partha, the wielder of the bow, there, surely, is righteousness, prosperity, victory and glory. That is my view.

*An offering *to* the Lord *of* pure knowledge itself, in a state of spiritual self-surrender, self-abnegation, self-effacement, enlightenment and integration of the mind.

Notes

[1]Brahmam is the ultimate reality and Maya is *anirvachaneeya*—indescribable.

Pure *Maya* or *Moola Prakriti* is infinite power, a state of perfect equilibrium with no differentiation or diversity When this undifferentiated state is disturbed, *Maya Sakti* emerges as the cause of all creations, and the Lord in his *Mayic* garb is referred to as one with a form (Saguna). So, when he is associated with Maya, he is Eswara.

And Maya is the Lord's power and *avidya* (ignorance) is our possession and this *avidya* creates a limited individuality in the Self (Jeevatman).

[2]The unseen Almighty, the Supreme without a name and form, the imperceptible one without any colour and taste is subtler than the subtlest. He is here, there, everywhere, within and without. And he is a 'Nirguna'—in that Supreme state without attributes.

When this transcendental being descends, of its own, from the unseen heights to assume a name and form, when this Supreme reality has a mission to fulfil for the sake of humanity, Lord, takes upon himself the task of protection of the good, promotion of righteousness (Dharma) and destruction of evil. He is then born in our midst. He is then in the Saguna aspect, when we worship him in this state of incarnation with a name and form.

[3]The result of Japa Yoga is the purification of the mind in which is reflected the Truth of one's Self. The more we surrender unto the Lord in this Japa Yoga activity, the greater will be our success.

A continuous process of chanting the Lord's name aids this art of Japa Yoga, which is also a part of the path of devotion (Bhakti).

In this path one occasionally meets those pursuing the path of knowledge (Jnana Marga) as well, because in its truest meaning and experience, one is inter-related to the other, and it is not separate from, or hostile to the allied wing.

There are no barriers to knowledge as such, and likewise no division as well, in true meditation or devotion.

But a tendency to doze, or to fly into a temper, or to become mechnical, or unduly reserved is there in a process of overdoing of Japa. One has to be wary of all this.

Therefore, a rosary (Japa Mala) helps in the initial stage. For every name of the particular God (Ishta Devata) that we chant 'mentally,' one bead of the rosary should be turned out with the middle finger allowing the index finger to stand apart.

In the midst of our Japa, if there is actually a mere turn of the beads without a chant of the holy name, we get alert and the mind is whipped up to proper action and correction. It will be realized that the chanting of the Lord's name and the turning of the bead in the Japa Mala synchronizes effortlessly after some time and that is the correct state: so, both the count and the thought should synchronize and go together.

No doubt we do Japa every day, but not probably for the purpose for which we should.

When we have made some progress and established ourselves in this art of Japa Yoga, we will find that it is easy to continue this practice even without a Japa Mala, which we first took up rather as an instrument for counter-balance until such time as we had steadied our position.

4What perishes is the body that is the perishable matter and the imperishable is the indestructible Self. By itself this body cannot act, and without this spark of life body is dead, *but* the self is *not* dead, inert, inactive or lifeless principle.

The spark of life which enlivens existence and illumines experiences is an undying immortal substratum. It is the pure consciousness which does not die when the body dies. In and out it pervades everything and exists everywhere. Here and now, it is in You, and in Me and right throughout it has a permanent stay.

The two are different—the one (body) born out of certain fluid combinations and the other, the Self (Atman) within, which defies death and all other descriptions.

5A person wanting to shift from an old house to a new one gets together all his belongings and keeps them all in a convenient place ready to depart at short notice. Similarly, in the case of a dying person, the five *karmendriyas* (motor organs) and the five Jnanendriyas (sense organs) become erratic in their functioning, and they start to shift their place only to stop functioning later.

Now begins the agonizing process of death. Physical inactivity, mental infirmity, a state of coma—the flow of life-current, generally, becomes inaudible. Now the subtle body of seventeen parts rests in the heart (*hri-*

daya kamala), ready to receive the departing signal. A final directive, a tip in the heart follows (*Marana Prakasikam*), when then the Life force goes out that way.

At the time of death, our past acts (karmas) act as the guiding star, a set of combination coming into a harmonious play with the last thoughts determining the type of birth, longevity and the sum total of the enjoyments of the future life—*Janma, Ayul,* and *Bhogam*—so says Sage Patanjali, in the Yoga Sutras

⁶There is an eightway approach to the path of devotion (Bhakti) as stated in the Bhakti Sutras. They are:

Sravanam—hearing about the Glory of the Lord

Kirtanam—singing his glory

Smaranam—remembering Him

Padasevanam—serving his lotus feet

Archanam—worshipping Him

Vandanam—prostrating before Him

Dasyam—service to him

Sakhyam—companionship with Him

Atmanivedanam—Surrender unto Him

In knowledge (Jnanam), the mind is dissolved in infinite Bliss, in Akhandananda, and in Bhakti, the mind is drowned in His infinite glory. In either case the limited individuality (Jeevatman) is lost and it becomes one with the Eternal.

⁷Love is divine in nature. It permeates as intrinsically as Truth, and exists as an attribute of that Absolute Reality. It sustains the beings and protects them, and in its light, birds gather unto flocks, animals into herds, and men are together in society.

Love is the warmth of life, and where fear chills, paralyzes and destroys; it stimulates, straightens and builds one to perfection and harmony.

Love is so inseparably bound to Divine nature that, when wafted by the magic wand of spirituality, it alleviates sufferings in this world of division, disharmony, diversity and plurality.

Love is blind to the dark and deluding outer unreal, but she, in her divine charm, is gracefully awake in the Light of our inner reality. There, we wonder at her divine beauty, and revel in her pristine purity.

It is this form of Pure Love, in its ecstatic heights and eccentric flow, that we see in the Gopis, love for Sri Krishna—womanhood weak and wavering.

⁸The light of the Sun illumines the objects of the world. Mere shedding

Notes

Light of my pure Consciousness must illumine them too, as it always, of course, does.

We all have the three states of existence—the waking, the dream and the deep sleep states. We all pass through the states of infancy, adulthood and old age and death, but these changes and experiences are for this physical body, but not for the changeless spirit behind, the Self (Atman).

The Pure Consciousness remains awake and illumines all the states and experiences of life in all this.

The Sun is not contaminated by the objects it illumines. The street light illumines those in wedding procession, and equally well those in a funeral party without getting itself involved either way. So too, the Self (Atman) the Light of Life, remains unaffected by the joys and sorrows of life.

The Atman is immortal and Thou art that. *Tat Tvam Asi.*

[9]Two birds bound to one another in close friendship are perched on the self-same tree. One of them eats the fruits of the tree with relish, whilst the other looks on without eating, like one indifferent.

Here, the reference is to the Jivatman, as the doer and enjoyer, identifying itself with the body, mind and intellect group, and the Paramatman as silent, unattached witness in its state of Pure consciousness, just merely looking on.

Therefore, the agency for actions and the enjoyment of the fruits of actions by the Jivatman are the superimpositions of the mind, whilst the real Self, the Paramatman, remains always as "an unseen seer" untainted by such modifications of the mind. He is the substratum on which other manifestations take place.

The waves are not different from the ocean, but yet, we generally consider them as separate, and treat the one as different from the other.

[10]Matter and spirit, the two aspects of the Lord (Eswara) are beginningless. In combination, they project creation, sustain it, and enact the scene of dissolution, and then repeat again thus.

All change belong to the realms of matter, and spirit is the changeless substratum (Kutasthan) in whose presence all such modifications take place. It is an unknown and uncaused cause: it is both the material and efficient cause for all mainfestations.

The destinies of matter become the tragic experience of the Spirit, *not* because they are in spirit, but because the changeless Self (higher) identifies itself with the lower group *i.e.* body-mind-intellect, and establishes an unholy and unhealthy contact.

So a state of

to spot out the real from the unreal, and to be rid of the saddening experiences of life i.e. *see* the rope as the rope only and not as a snake, *see* the post as post only and not as a ghost, *see* the high waves as the ocean only and not as waves that rise and fall, and *see* the mirage as mirage only and not as a sheet of water.

[11]Maha Yuga, the rotation of the giant wheel of time and creation, consists of 4,380,000 years. It is divided into four smaller cyclone:

Krita Yoga of 1,752,000 years, Treta of 1,314,000 years, Dwapara of 876,000 years and Kali of 438,000 years.

Krita Yuga may be compared to the break of day, that fosters contemplation and devotion.

Treta is the beginning of the day, suitable for acquisition of knowledge and wealth.

Dwapara corresponds to the latter part of the day, suitable for offering and the like.

Kali, which is the present one, is the dark period of the day, when the right and the wrong are not clear, and when mankind departs from the path of Dharma (righteousness). In this age of Kali, charity and offering with love and fervour (Dana) are the greatest virtues.

We are now in the 5078th year of the Kali Yuga.

[12]The great law of Karma, governing both the working of the universe and the individuals in all stages—the universe during its emergenee, manifestation and disintegration and the individual beings in their different lives, with the inexorable law of cause and effect . . .

There is an equal and opposite reaction to every action, and for every cause there is an effect, and the effect, in turn, produces its own ripple—yet another cause. This chain remains unbroken, until consiousness breaks it down.

So, if the conditions in which a certain cause was introduced remains the same, the same effect would have to be produced by the same cause, whenever it operates, or repeats in future.

The Philosophy of the Science of practical action is to dismember the cause and thus be rewarded and redeemed, as a snake does its slough; otherwise one is bound.

Within the framework of the Law, man is a master of his destiny: he is neither punished nor rewarded for his deeds by the Creator, as this is being so done, *only* by his own deeds under the Law, with the Lord as an overall witness (Karmadhyaksha).

Finally, this scheme is designed not to deter one in his path, but to help him develop a scheme, and to evolve him to attain cosmic Consciousness, and bondage.

[13]Freedom to act is there for all, at all times. The power of free will is denied to none and Hinduism is not a religion of the fatalists. One may decide to perform or not an action in respect of which a thought wave has already arisen in his mind. Whilst he may choose the right path or the wrong one, and go his own way exercising his free will, fate intervenes as a predetermined factor to offer its fruits of action.

Though *prarabdha* is the dispenser of the fruits of action, it is not always the controller of our destiny: for we have the free will too; and by repeated right actions we can give a new direction to the type of *prarabdha* that is going to be in store for us.

So free will is always there, and fate intervenes only when one is destined to suffer that. Also, in regard to free will generally the type of action one indulges in, is related to the thoughts he has developed, which, in turn, is the outcome of the tendencies and latent desires (vasanas).

The scriptures say that in spite of all that has been said, actions and inaction are difficult to be fully and precisely defined.

[14]*Prarabdha* exists as a set-group and combination; and only a part of the well stored effects of actions (*Prarabdha*) starts to bear fruit in the present life giving us this birth and the rest of the *Prarabdha* is unutilized (latent), as though un-tapped.

Sanchita is the effect of all acts done in this life uptil this moment and *Agami* are the effects of all acts that we might do in this life in future. Unless they are allowed to pass over to the side of *prarabdha* progressively as they do, otherwise in the fire of true knowledge, the *sanchita* and *agami* Karmas only are destroyed—not the *prarabdha* which has to be exhausted for there is no other course enlightened with knowledge (Jnanis) have to work this out. The working of *prarabdha karma* in this life which cannot be destroyed, is therefore compared to the going round of a potter's wheel, because it has already started with life and has to run its course. So *prarabdha* in this respect is different from *sanchita* and *agami*.

[15]The physical functions of the body are carried on by five principal divisions of vital energy (Prana). There are also five minor divisions of Prana known as the *upa pranas*. The main Pranas are:

Prana—the life breath functioning in the lungs and respiratory organs, in the eyes, ear, mouth and nose: this also engages the other pranas differently.

Apana: It works in the colon and bladder—in the excretory and genital organs.

Samana—it performs its course in the digestive system.

Udana—it is perceptible in the larynx and produces sound and leads the embodied Soul to the world of the virtuous or sinful ones.

Vyana—it expresses itself in blood circulation and in the nerve currents. Of the Atman is born this Prana, but Prana is *not* the Soul.

Prana is not also the life-breath, because breathing is just one of the many activities of this vital force, but like the shadow of a man the Atman spreads itself out on all that.

The Sun is verily the external Prana. He rises gracing the prana in the eyes.

No mortal ever lives by Prana or Apana alone, for, the Soul is the Prana of all Pranas.

[16]Jnana Yajna is an offering of pure knowledge itse'f directed initially towards disinterested enquiry and pursuit, and ultimately for a consummation of that paramount state in which You are Your Own, stripped of all physical, mental and intellectual afflictions. It is a total offering of the mind and its products.

[17]The Guru is an enlightened Mahatman who has an honoured place in the religious of the world. Great veneration is to be shown to this saviour of the Soul.

We respect the learned, but we worship the Guru, because he is not a mere teacher of the sciences of this mundane words. He is one who, soaked in the experience of the Self, is exceptionally qualified to initiate the disciple in the path of Atma Vidya.

He creates the fire of knowledge in us (Brahma Jnana)—so he is (Brahma): helps us sustain same (Vishnu): and in the light of the true knowledge (Atma Vidya) destroys ignorance (Maheswara).

Talks, discourses, declarations and sermons are excellent media for expressions of the outer world knowledge, but when one has to "talk to oneself in the silent language of the Self," a Guru alone can teach us that sacred and secret knowledge, and lead us from darkness to light.

[18]Meditation is a process by which, to the exclusion of all other thoughts we attain a continuity of thought of a single-pointed nature which generates a powerful energy and strengthens our efforts towards spiritual progress. It helps to drop off the lower values of life, and by lifting our ideals up, we are led to the ultimate goal of self-realization.

Sat Sang (association with the pious and good natured) and 'satvic' food help us discipline the mind which, in turn, creates for us a meditative mood, sure enough to achieve victory and bold enough to repulse the onslaughts of the outer world objects.

[19]In this state of self-realization they experience the dissolution of

identity and the conditioning of the ego-state. This is the pure and primal state of one's awakening to Atman in its ultimate state.

²⁰The Jivan Mukta is a liberated Soul on earth. He can be here in our midst. He is an enlightened Mahatman who has fulfilled the mission of his Life. He does not mistake the body-mind-intellect group as his Self. He is one who has destroyed the superimposed limitations on his Infinite Being. He is His own, a king of kings, and also like a king who has regained his kingdom after exile.

He may outwardly appear to be a lunatic, a rustic or a child to the worldly minded, but actually he is the wise among men, and one who is awake to what we are dead, and dead to what we hanker after.

Seated in Truth, he remains unidentified with the fleeting experiences of life. Merged with the infinite, he loses his identity in this world of plurality and mortality.

His *avidya* (ignorance) is destroyed by the fire knowledge, and he casts off his physical body when the *prarabdha karma* comes to an end.

Wherever he *lives* he is a *Jivanmukta*, and wherever he may *die* he has a deathless existence with the Infinite.

²¹Sravanam is the hearing of the spiritual truths from those learned.

Mananam is the next stage of brooding over the same, so as to be clear and certain of what has been heard with their doubts dispelled ... and

Nidhidyasanam is the actual practice and pursuit of what has been heard, and finally ascertained in a state of Mananam, as the objective to be achieved. These three are the important stages which a seeker after Truth has to tread in the path of Knowledge.

²²Yoga effectively activates, integrates, invigourates and finally sublimates our thoughts, movements, actions (Karma) knowledge (Jnana) intellect (Buddhi) and devotion (Bhakti). It is the only potent solvent which can effectively change the very base, composition and complexion of the dull substance of life which, otherwise by itself, can't solve the problems of life here and hereafter.

²³Brahmam is all-pervading, and these is no place where He is not. He, being everywhere, sees all, knows all and encompasses all.

Being pure, the principle of Maya is absent in him. He is radiant, and because of the purity of his existence, there is a brilliance which dispels the darkness of ignorance and a glow which lits up the torch of true knowledge.

In the Pure wisdom He reveals, there is no room for doubt and ignorance. In the Oneness of Truth He is, there is no place for inequality. Instead, it is immortality which one attains.

He is all, and yet he remains apart, as a silent witness, aloof, and un-crushed by the weight of the other world happenings. What a wonder!

[24]Actually, the greater happiness Bliss, is the essential, inherent nature of one's own Self (Atman) . . . Sat Chit Anandam. It is there with every-one ever, whether one strives for it or not: is extrovert or introvert—two positions: one whose mind is just simply not drawn away, and one who is ahead a bit, i.e. is in actual introspective experience. The end result from one point of view ultimately is the same although it is indicated as diffe-rent in the two cases above of two different states or experience.

[25]Here "food" may be taken for the worldly objects and 'relish' for desires. Absence of both i.e. the worldly objects and desires is not actual death for spiritual aspirants, because impermanency, birth and death are only for the objects and experiences in this created world and for the body but not for the Self (Atman)—the deathless unborn one which is entirely different from this body.

So this paramount everlasting state other than the mundane existence is attained by renunciation or relinquishment of both 'food and relish' i.e. the sense objects and desire too.

[26]A Sage or Muni is an adept in the act of *manana* . . . and *manana* is brooding over the spiritual truths that have been heard, so as to be clear and certain of what has been heard, with their doubts dispelled "for a ready entrance into the Halls of practice, peace and experience, and for a vision of the Self." It is a state of detachment, of silent introspection of a self analysis of men, matters and phenomena, both material and spiritual.

[27]This statement can be taken to mean "even when you are starved of the outer world experiences" and when you are moving about in the world on that account, as a living dead for all outward appearances.

[28]The Pranava is the mystic syllable or a symbol of the Atman which pervades our life and runs through our very breath (prana). There is nothing that is not encompassed by it.

This Sylable is both microcosmic and macrocosmic, is the cause and effect, is the past, present and future, and this Pranava is also that which transcends the divisions of time.

There is an identification of the three states of existence i.e. waking, dream and the deep sleep states with the three parts of Om (A U M) which is verily our Self. The waking and dream states seem to subsist in, and emerge from, the deep sleep state.

But this monosyllable in its partless aspect, is the Self (Atman), and by Pranavopasana, or the meditation on the Self, one realizes the Supreme Truth that All is the Self.

29The mind is more powerful than the Man. It is the cause for our bondage and liberation. It is ever unsteady and never calm. In short, without a mind, a man does not exist, nor does this world for him. But it is only when the extrovert thoughts of the mind are controlled and in this path Yoga aids the process of integration of the Soul and the mind.

In Samadhi there is an oneness of the concentrated mind with the contemplated Self, and a continuous experience of the self-revealed Ananda. It is not a state of non-existence, but of Supreme Bliss (Paramananda), a rare and pure variety of a re-discovered Self in its immortal glory.

Here, the mind does not find out Brahman, or create a state of Bliss. Instead, when the egocentric mind dies, the outward search for Truth ends to give birth to the infinitude of the Self within, which automatically reveals itself just as the Sun, when the could moves away.

30The Horse and the chariot. In the Upanisads this body is likened to a chariot with the soul as Master. The intellect is the charioteer, and the mind the rein. The horses are the sense-organs (Jnanendriyas and Karmendrias). The roads on which this chariot (body) runs are the sense objects.

The sense organs (horses) are uncontrollable like the brute horses in the case of a person lacking self-control, whereas they are like the good horses of an able charioteer if one is disciplined and well regulated in his life and pursuits.

So, train the charioteer, for the must be sane and sober if he has to reach the destination safely after a happy journey.